BLUE-RIBBON
COOKIES

ALSO BY MARIA POLUSHKIN ROBBINS

The Cook's Quotation Book
The Dumpling Cookbook
Blue-Ribbon Pies
Blue-Ribbon Pickles & Preserves

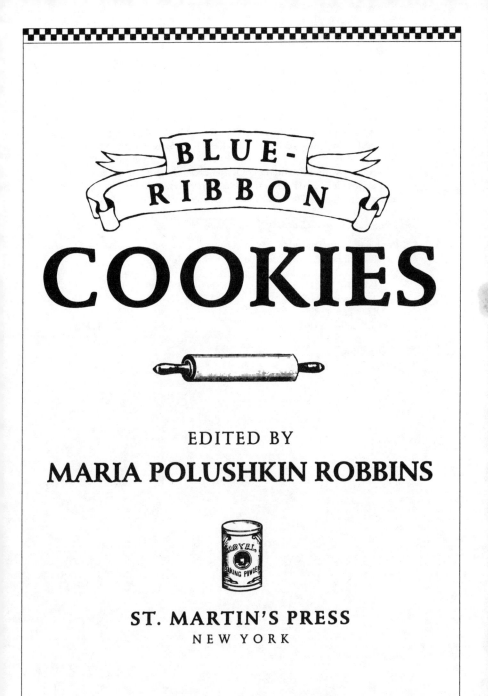

BLUE-RIBBON

COOKIES

EDITED BY

MARIA POLUSHKIN ROBBINS

ST. MARTIN'S PRESS

NEW YORK

Library of Congress Cataloging-in-Publication Data

Robbins, Maria Polushkin
    Blue ribbon cookies / by Maria Polushkin Robbins.
        p. cm.
    ISBN 0-312-01738-3   ISBN 0-312-01739-1 (pbk.)
    1. Cookies.   I. Title.
    TX772.P65 1988
    641.8'654—dc19   87-38272
                                                              CIP

First Edition
10 9 8 7 6 5 4 3 2 1

Contents

Acknowledgments

Though I worked alone on this project, I was, by mail and phone, connected with hundreds of people all over the country. I sent out so many letters that the local postal clerk groaned when he saw me coming, and I received so many responses that my mailman staggered under the load. This book would not have happened without the generous help of the officers of the state and regional fair organizations and without the cooks themselves who shared their recipes with me and readers of this book. My heartfelt thanks to them all. Thanks, too, to Jim Charlton and Barbara Binswanger, and to Barbara Anderson, my editor, who was patient and helpful; and, finally, thanks to my husband Ken, who helped stuff all those envelopes.

Introduction

There is something "just right" about a cookie. They are easy to make, portable, durable, don't need refrigeration, and won't melt in your hand or go stale overnight. They can be a snack, a reward, a gift, or even, as with Sesame Street's Cookie Monster, an obsession. But above all, a cookie is the quintessential treat. Small wonder that every lunch box, picnic basket, or after-school snack provides a bigger smile when it includes a cookie or two, preferably homemade.

"Homemade" is the word that commands the emotions and loyalties of every cookie fan. Supermarkets may devote entire aisles to the display of cookies—from the plainest wafers to the most exotic concoctions of nuts, chocolates, and spices—yet nothing substitutes for the taste or emotional satisfaction of a homemade cookie, still warm from the oven.

The irresistible appeal of homemade cookies is a secret that has not escaped America's contest-oriented cooks. As I was collecting recipes for my two previous Blue-Ribbon cookbooks, people kept sending me cookie recipes, unsolicited, right along with the pie and preserves recipes I'd requested. They would write notes like, "Here's my deep-dish apple pie recipe, but the recipe that the judges *really* love is this one, for my double-chocolate brownies," or my Brazil nut bars, or whatever.

Just as the recipes in this book have won the admiration of the most demanding of tasters, so, too, will they win the praise of family and friends. Each of the book's 100 recipes—from Iced Cherry Gems to Coconut Clouds, to Pumpkin Chocolate Chips and Black Walnut Wonder Cookies—is a top prize winner, guaranteed to bring the best of homemade flavor to your kitchen and cookie jar.

Tips for Baking Great Cookies

Cookies are probably the easiest things to make in a kitchen this side of peanut butter sandwiches, and they are certainly the most widely appreciated and the most frequent objects of unauthorized sampling, too. Even if you've never baked anything in your whole life, you can still bake great cookies. You won't need a lot of fancy equipment, exotic ingredients, or any special training. And though the variety of cookie recipes may seem bewilderingly large, they all more or less come down to just six basic types:

Bar cookies are the simplest of all. Made in one piece in a cake or jelly roll pan, then cut into bars or squares after they've baked and cooled, they have a cakelike texture that is moist and rich. Often they're topped with icing or frosting. When you're short on time but want to serve a home-baked cookie, these are the ones to make.

Drop cookies are made by dropping mounds of soft dough from a teaspoon onto a cookie sheet. Use two teaspoons, one to hold the dough, the other to scoop it off. Drop cookies can be either soft or crisp in texture, and they often contain pieces of chocolate, fruit, and/or nuts. They do tend to spread out during baking, so it's important to space them at least two inches apart on the baking sheet. If the dough seems very soft to you and spreads too quickly, just refrigerate it for thirty minutes or so.

Molded or shaped cookies are usually crisp in texture. The dough is often refrigerated for a while for easier handling, then the hands are used to shape or mold it into balls. The balls can then be flattened with the bottom of a water glass that has been dipped in sugar, or with the tines of a fork. In some recipes the cookies are dipped in sugar or nuts before baking. In others a depression is made with the thumb, to be filled later with jam or icing.

Refrigerator or ice box cookies are perfect if you are busy but organized. Make the dough at your leisure and keep it on hand in the refrigerator or freezer to slice and bake whenever you want. The dough is shaped into a log, wrapped in plastic or wax paper, and chilled for at least two hours or overnight. The roll is cut into thin slices and baked on a greased cookie sheet. Refrigerator cookie dough will keep for about a week in the refrigerator and longer in the freezer. These have a good crisp texture.

Rolled cookies are rolled out with a rolling pin on a lightly floured surface and cut into any shape with a knife, a glass, or any special cookie cutter. If you find yourself with a cookie dough that's sticky and difficult to handle, roll it out between two sheets of wax paper. The thinner the dough is rolled, the crisper the cookie. Rolled cookies can be decorated with sugar, raisins, and icing.

Pressed or piped cookies are often considered special occasion cookies because of their intricate shapes and decorative appearance. The soft dough is refrigerated for body, then pressed through a cookie press or piped through a pastry bag, often fitted with a star-shaped tube.

Equipment **Cookie sheets.** The most important qualification for a cookie sheet is that it fit comfortably inside your oven. At least two inches all around is important for good air circulation. Otherwise, let your personal preference and pocketbook be your guide, but the heaviest sheets are the best. Many have a nonstick surface. If you use these, ignore directions to grease cookie sheets before baking. Some cooks recommend lining cookie sheets with aluminum foil. In that case be sure to grease the foil with butter or margarine if called for. The foil method has many advantages, not the least of which is that cleanup is a cinch. Then, too, you can prepare sheets of foil, assembly-line style, so that as each batch of cookies comes from the oven, you slip them off and slide a fresh batch in their place.

An alternative to aluminum foil is baking parchment paper. It's coated with silicone and eliminates the need for greasing.

Measuring cups and spoons.   It's always a good idea to have an assortment of graduated measuring cups on hand for dry ingredients. Use glass measuring cups with clear markings for liquid ingredients. A set of spoons should allow you easily to measure out anything from a quarter teaspoon to a tablespoon.

Flour sifter

Small and large mixing bowls

An electric mixer.   The big fancy ones are great, but a small, inexpensive hand-held model will work just as well.

Mixing spoons and scrapers.   I prefer wooden spoons and rubber scrapers.

Rolling pin

Cookie cutters

Cookie press with an assortment of disks.
Instead of a cookie press, you might prefer a pastry bag with an assortment of tips.

An accurate timer

Metal spatula.   Use this for removing cookies from the cookie sheet.

Wire racks.   These are useful for cooling cookies quickly so they stay crisp.

About Ingredients

- Use all-purpose flour unless otherwise specified.
- Butter or margarine? Many cooks feel that there is no substitute for butter because it does taste better. Margarine is healthier and cheaper. You decide. All the butter called for is unsalted (sweet) butter.
- Butter, margarine, and vegetable shortening should be at room temperature unless otherwise specified.
- Sugar when called for in a recipe is white granulated sugar. Other sugars, such as brown or confectioners' sugar, are specified as such. Confectioners' sugar is another name for powdered sugar.
- Honey, molasses, and corn syrup are used in some of the recipes. Do not substitute ordinary sugar.
- All eggs are "large" unless otherwise specified.
- Cocoa is unsweetened cocoa powder.

Making the Cookies

- Read through the recipe to see if you need to allow time for chilling the dough. Adjust your schedule accordingly.
- Prepare cookie sheets or baking pan.
- The first step is often to cream butter (or margarine or shortening) together with sugar. This is impossible to do if butter is cold; it must be softened to room temperature. Creaming can be done by hand with a large wooden spoon, but is much easier with an electric mixer. Creaming, mixing, and blending are all done at medium speed. Always cream butter and sugar together until mixture is smooth, light, and fluffy.
- When flour is added to the creamed mixture, mix just until everything is well blended. Overmixing makes the dough tough.

- Place cookie dough on cool cookie sheets. Cookie sheets still hot from the oven should be run under cold water, dried, and greased (if called for) before arranging the next batch, even if using foil.

- Know your oven and adjust baking times accordingly. Check cookies a few minutes before the minimum baking time called for. Cookies burn quickly. Here are a few things to look for: Bar cookies are done when a toothpick inserted in the center comes out clean. Drop and molded cookies are done when a finger pressed on the surface leaves a slight indentation. Rolled and refrigerator cookies are done when they are just turning a golden brown. Pressed cookies should be firm and just slightly brown around the edges.

- Almost all cookies, except bar cookies, should be removed with a spatula to a wire rack to cool. Bar cookies should be left in the pan and set on a wire rack to cool.

Almond Butter Cookies

These are: molded cookies
You will need: greased cookie sheet

¼ **pound butter or margarine, softened to room temperature**
½ **cup almond butter, available in health food stores**
½ **cup sugar**
½ **cup brown sugar**
1 **egg**
1¼ **cups flour**
½ **teaspoon baking powder**
¾ **teaspoon baking soda**
¼ **teaspoon salt**
Finely chopped almonds for topping

Cream together butter or margarine and almond butter until light and fluffy. Add sugars and beat until smooth, then beat in egg. Sift together flour, baking powder, baking soda, and salt. Stir into creamed mixture. Chill dough for several hours.

Preheat oven to 375°F.

Shape dough into 1¾-inch balls and place 3 inches apart on lightly greased cookie sheet. Flatten crisscross style with a fork dipped in flour. Sprinkle with chopped almonds. Bake for 10 to 12 minutes. Cool on wire racks.

Yield: about 3 dozen

Loretta Arter
Madera,
California
Madera
District Fair

Grandmother's Anise Cookies

Great at Christmastime and every other time as well!

These are: molded cookies
You will need: greased cookie sheet

¼ **pound butter, softened to room temperature**
1¼ **cups sugar**
2 **eggs**
6 **tablespoons milk**
3¼ **cups flour**
1 **teaspoon baking soda**
1 **teaspoon cream of tartar**
½ **teaspoon of salt**
2 **tablespoons aniseed**
Confectioners' sugar

Cream together butter and sugar until light and fluffy. Beat in eggs and milk. Sift together flour, baking soda, cream of tartar and salt. Stir into creamed mixture and mix well. Stir in aniseed. Chill dough in refrigerator for at least 3 hours.

Preheat oven to 350°F.

Shape dough into 1-inch balls and roll in confectioners' sugar. Place on greased cookie sheet 2 inches apart. Bake for about 8 minutes, or until cookies are golden. Cool on wire racks.

Yield: about 6½ dozen

Mrs. Alberta
Fahrenbach
Muncy,
Pennsylvania
Hughsville Fair
Lycoming County

Apple Oatmeal Cookies

These are: filled drop cookies
You will need: greased cookie sheet

Apple Filling

1 cup finely diced peeled apple
½ cup raisins
¼ cup chopped walnuts
½ cup sugar
2 tablespoons water
1 teaspoon cinnamon
¼ teaspoon nutmeg

Combine all the ingredients in a small saucepan. Cook over medium heat, stirring frequently, until the apple is tender and mixture is thick, about 10 minutes. Remove from heat and let cool.

½ pound butter or margarine, softened to
room temperature
1 cup brown sugar
2 eggs
2 cups sifted flour
2 teaspoons baking powder
½ teaspoon salt
1 teaspoon cinnamon
½ teaspoon ground cloves
½ cup milk
2 cups quick-cooking rolled oats

Preheat oven to 375°F.

Cream together butter and brown sugar until fluffy. Beat in eggs. Sift together flour, baking powder, salt, cinnamon, and cloves; add to creamed mixture alternately with milk. Stir in rolled oats. Set aside ¾ cup of the dough. Drop remainder by teaspoonfuls onto greased cookie sheet. Make a small depression in the center of each cookie. Top with apple filling and a small amount of reserved dough. Bake for 8 to 10 minutes. Cool on wire racks.

Yield: 3 dozen

Ruth B. Ekberg
Reedley, California
Fresno District Fair

Apricot Cheese Cookies

These are: filled rolled cookies
You will need: ungreased cookie sheet

¼ pound butter or margarine, softened to
   room temperature
1 cup grated sharp cheese
1⅓ cups sifted flour
2 tablespoons water
1 cup dried apricots
2 cups water
1 cup sugar
½ cup raisins

Cream together butter and cheese until light and fluffy. Blend sifted flour into creamed mixture. Add 2 tablespoons water and mix well. Cover and chill for 4 hours.

Cook apricots with 2 cups water over medium heat until apricots are soft. Drain well and stir sugar into hot fruit. Return to saucepan and cook, stirring, over low heat until mixture boils and becomes smooth. Remove from heat and stir in raisins. Let cool.

Preheat oven to 375°F.

Divide chilled dough in half. Roll each half out to a 10-inch square on a lightly floured surface. Cut rolled dough into 2½-inch squares. Place 1 teaspoon apricot filling in middle of each square. Bring up diagonal corners and seal. Repeat with the remaining dough. Bake on ungreased cookie sheet for 8 to 10 minutes. Cool on wire racks.

Ruth B. Ekberg
Reedley, California
Fresno District Fair

Yield: 2½ dozen

Apricot Pastries

These cookies are unusual in that they use yeast as leavening. The dough rises while the cookies bake. They contain almost no sugar and are sweetened by the apricot filling and the final dusting of confectioners' sugar.

These are: filled rolled cookies
You will need: greased cookie sheet

2 cups dried apricots
2 cups water
½ cup milk
1 package active dry yeast
1 egg, slightly beaten
½ teaspoon vanilla extract
3 cups sifted flour
1 tablespoon sugar
½ teaspoon salt
1 cup vegetable shortening
Confectioners' sugar for topping

Simmer the apricots in water until tender and mixture is thick (about 30 minutes). Let cool. Scald the milk and let cool until it is just warm to the touch. Stir in yeast and let soften. Add egg and vanilla to yeast mixture. Sift together flour, sugar, and salt, then cut in the shortening until mixture resembles coarse crumbs. Stir in yeast mixture and mix well.

Preheat oven to 350°F.

Divide dough into four parts. Roll out each piece of dough on a board that has been well dusted with confectioners' sugar. Roll each piece out until it is approximately 10 inches square. Cut each large square into 16 2-inch squares. Place a heaping teaspoon of apricots in the center of each 2-inch square on a diagonal line. Pinch two opposite corners together. Place 2 inches apart on a greased cookie sheet. Let stand 10 minutes. Bake for 10 to 12 minutes. Remove at once from sheet and cool on wire racks under which you have placed sheets of wax paper. While cookies are still warm, sprinkle with confectioners' sugar.

Yield: about 5 dozen

Lanelle Rhoads
Phoenix, Arizona
Arizona State Fair

Apricot Spice Bars with Lemon Glaze

These are: bar cookies
You will need: greased 15 × 10 × 1-inch baking pan

⅓ cup vegetable shortening
1½ cups brown sugar
½ cup honey
3 eggs
1¾ cups flour
1 teaspoon baking powder
1 teaspoon salt
1 teaspoon cinnamon
½ teaspoon ground cloves
1 6-ounce package dried apricots, finely chopped
1 cup chopped nuts

Preheat oven to 350°F.

Cream together shortening, sugar and honey. Beat in eggs. Sift together flour, baking powder, salt, cinnamon, and cloves. Add to creamed mixture and stir well. Fold in apricots and nuts. Spread in a greased 15 × 10 × 1-inch baking pan. Bake for 20 to 25 minutes. Cool in pan on wire rack. Brush with Lemon Glaze. Cut into squares.

Lemon Glaze   ¾ cup confectioners' sugar
1 tablespoon lemon juice

Mix sugar and lemon juice to make a glaze.

Yield: about 3 dozen

Helen L. Hannon
Kouts, Indiana
Porter County Fair

Best Brownies

These are: bar cookies
You will need: greased 9 × 13-inch pan

¼ **pound butter**
½ **cup cocoa**
2 **cups sugar**
4 **eggs**
2 **teaspoons vanilla extract**
1½ **cups flour**
¼ **teaspoon salt**
1 **cup flaked coconut**

Preheat oven to 350°F.

Melt the butter, pour into a large mixing bowl, and beat in cocoa and sugar. When mixture is smooth, beat in eggs, one at a time, then vanilla. Stir in flour, salt, and coconut. Pour into a greased 9 × 13-inch pan and bake for 25 minutes. Let cool in pan on racks and cut into squares.

Yield: about 30

Mrs. Eldon
Wichmann
St. Libory,
Nebraska
Howard
County Fair

Brownies with Creamy Brownie Frosting

These are: bar cookies
You will need: greased and floured 9-inch square pan

¼ pound butter, melted
1 cup sugar
1 teaspoon vanilla extract
2 eggs
½ cup flour
⅓ cup cocoa
¼ teaspoon baking powder
¼ teaspoon salt
½ cup chopped walnuts

Preheat oven 350°F.

In a mixing bowl, blend butter, sugar, and vanilla extract. Beat in eggs, one at a time. Sift together flour, cocoa, baking powder, and salt and stir into liquid ingredients. Stir in nuts. Pour into a greased and floured 9-inch square pan. Bake for 20 to 25 minutes. Cool in pan on rack. Frost with Creamy Brownie Frosting. When cool, cut into squares.

Creamy Brownie Frosting

3 tablespoons butter, softened to
    room temperature
½ teaspoon vanilla extract
2 tablespoons cocoa
1 tablespoon light corn syrup
1 to 2 tablespoons milk
1 cup confectioners' sugar

Cream together butter, vanilla, cocoa, and corn syrup. Beat in milk and confectioners' sugar. Beat until mixture is a spreading consistency.

Janice F. Virgo
Delhi, California
Stanislaus
County Fair

Yield: about 16

Double Chocolate Brownies

Mrs. Plante writes that this prizewinning recipe came from a Gold Medal flour bag, and she made some changes to her own taste.

These are: bar cookies
You will need: greased 9-inch square pan

¾ cup flour
¼ teaspoon baking soda
¼ teaspoon salt
⅓ cup butter
½ cup sugar
2 tablespoons water
1 12-ounce package (2 cups) semisweet
    chocolate morsels
1 teaspoon vanilla extract
2 eggs
1 cup chopped walnuts

Preheat oven 325°F.

Sift together flour, baking soda, and salt; reserve. Combine butter, sugar, and water in a medium saucepan and bring just to the boil. Remove from heat. Add 1½ cups of the chocolate morsels and vanilla. Stir until chocolate melts and mixture is smooth. Transfer to a large bowl. Beat in eggs, one at a time. Gradually blend in flour mixture. Stir in remaining ½ cup chocolate morsels and the nuts. Spread in a greased 9-inch square pan and bake for 25 to 30 minutes. Cool in pan on rack, then cut into squares.

Yield: about 16

Carolyn G. Plante
Ceres, California
Stanislaus
County Fair and
Alameda
County Fair

Fudge Cinnamon Brownies

These are: bar cookies
You will need: greased 15½ × 10½ × 1-inch jelly roll pan

2 cups flour
2 cups sugar
½ pound butter or margarine
7 tablespoons cocoa
1 cup water
½ cup plain yogurt, at room temperature
2 eggs
1 teaspoon vanilla extract
1 teaspoon baking soda
1 teaspoon ground cinnamon
1 cup chopped pecans

Preheat oven to 400°F.

Sift together flour and sugar into a bowl. Combine butter, cocoa, and water in a heavy saucepan. Bring to a boil over medium heat and stir to blend. Slowly pour hot mixture over flour and sugar, blending with an electric mixer. Add yogurt, eggs, vanilla, baking soda, and cinnamon. Mix well. Spread in a greased 15½ × 10½ × 1-inch jelly roll pan. Bake for 20 minutes, or until a toothpick inserted in center comes out clean. Cool in pan on rack. Frost with Chocolate Fudge Frosting. Sprinkle with chopped pecans. Cut into 2-inch squares.

Yield: 35 squares

Chocolate ¼ **pound butter or margarine**
Fudge 5 **tablespoons cocoa**
Frosting 6 **tablespoons milk**
1 **pound confectioners' sugar**
1 **teaspoon vanilla extract**

Melt butter in a large (2-quart) heavy saucepan. Add cocoa and milk. Stir well. Bring mixture to a boil and remove from heat. Add confectioners' sugar and vanilla. Beat until smooth.

Blanche Falk
Louisville,
Kentucky
Kentucky State
Fair

Black Walnut Wonder Cookies

"This is a favorite chocolate cookie recipe from my great aunt," writes Connie Betz, who has won many prizes at the Tri-County Fair in Mendota, Illinois.

These are: drop cookies
You will need: ungreased cookie sheet

¼ pound butter, softened to room temperature
1 cup sugar
3 tablespoons cocoa
2 eggs
½ cup milk
2 cups flour
1 teaspoon baking soda
1 cup chopped black walnuts

Preheat oven to 350°F.
   Cream butter and sugar together. Stir in cocoa. Beat eggs lightly and stir into butter-sugar mixture. Stir in milk. Sift together flour and baking soda, then stir into liquid mixture. Blend well. Fold in the nuts. Drop by teaspoonfuls onto ungreased cookie sheets. Bake for 8 to 10 minutes. Let cool in pan on wire racks, then frost.

Frosting 2 tablespoons butter, softened to
       room temperature
  2½ cups confectioners' sugar
  2½ tablespoons cocoa
  5 tablespoons or more cream or milk
  Walnut halves, for topping

Mix all the ingredients, except walnut halves to a spreadable consistency. Frost cookies and place a walnut half on each.

Yield: about 3 dozen

Connie L. Betz
Compton, Illinois
Tri-County Fair

Brazil Nut Bars

These are: bar cookies
You will need: greased and floured 9-inch-square pan

4 tablespoons butter, cold
1 cup sifted flour
½ teaspoon salt
¾ cup light brown sugar
2 eggs, beaten
2 cups finely chopped Brazil nuts
½ cup flaked coconut
¼ teaspoon coconut extract
¾ teaspoon vanilla extract
1 cup semisweet chocolate morsels
¼ cup light corn syrup
1 tablespoon water

Preheat oven to 375°F.

Blend butter, flour, and ¼ teaspoon salt and press this mixture into a 9-inch square pan that has been well greased and floured. Bake for 15 minutes.

Meanwhile, beat sugar into eggs. Add remaining salt, 1 cup of Brazil nuts, flaked coconut, coconut extract, and vanilla. Spread over baked layer and return to oven to bake for 15 minutes longer. Let cool. Melt chocolate in the top of a double boiler, then stir in corn syrup and water. Spread on cooled layers and sprinkle with remaining 1 cup nuts. Let stand until topping is firm, then cut into bars.

Yield: 16 to 20

Patricia Leinweber
Phoenix, Arizona
Arizona State Fair

Brown Edge Wafers

"These are reminiscent of those we used to buy years ago," says Marion Flynn. "I developed it by trial and error and it's very simple." Delicious, too.

These are: molded cookies
You will need: greased cookie sheet

½ **cup vegetable shortening**
¼ **pound butter, softened to room temperature**
1 **cup sugar**
1 **egg**
2 **cups flour**
Additional granulated sugar

Cream together the shortening, butter, and sugar. Beat in egg. Stir in flour to blend. Chill cookie mixture in refrigerator until firm.

Preheat oven to 350°F.

Shape mixture into 1-inch balls and place them 2 inches apart on a greased cookie sheet. Wrap a small glass in a damp cloth. Dip bottom of glass (cloth) in granulated sugar and flatten each ball by pressing down on it with the bottom of the glass. Bake for about 10 minutes, until there is a light golden edge around each cookie. Cool on wire racks.

Yield: 4 dozen

Marion Flynn
West Falmouth,
Massachusetts
Barnstable
County Fair

Buttermilk Cinnamon Bars

These are: bar cookies
You will need: greased 9 × 13-inch pan

1 ¼ cups sugar
¾ cup brown sugar
2 cups flour
½ cup vegetable shortening, at room temperature
½ cup shredded coconut
½ cup nuts
1 egg, well beaten
½ teaspoon salt
1 teaspoon cinnamon
1 teaspoon baking powder
1 cup buttermilk
1 teaspoon vanilla extract

Preheat oven to 350°F.

Blend sugars, flour, and shortening together until mixture resembles coarse meal. (Can be done in a food processor.) Combine 2 cups of this mixture with coconut and nuts. Press lightly into a greased 9 × 13-inch pan. Combine all the remaining ingredients and mix well. Spread over first layer and bake for 45 minutes. While still warm, frost with a thin confectioners' sugar icing (page 122). Cool in pan on wire rack and cut into bars.

Yield: about 4 dozen

Helen L. Hannon
Kouts, Indiana
Porter County Fair

Butterscotch Refrigerator Cookies

These are: refrigerator cookies
You will need: ungreased cookie sheet

1 cup vegetable shortening
2 cups brown sugar
2 eggs
2 tablespoons sour milk or plain yogurt
1 teaspoon vanilla extract
3 cups flour
1 teaspoon salt
1 teaspoon baking powder
1 teaspoon baking soda
1 cup chopped nuts

Cream together the shortening and sugar until smooth. Beat in eggs, one at a time, then sour milk and vanilla. Sift together the flour, salt, baking powder, and baking soda. Stir into creamed mixture. Stir in chopped nuts. Divide in half, roll into logs, wrap in plastic, and chill in refrigerator until firm.

Preheat oven to 350°F.

Cut logs into slices ⅛ inch thick and bake, 2 inches apart, on ungreased cookie sheet for 8 to 10 minutes. Cool on wire racks.

Yield: about 80

Louise
Schneiderman
Bottineau,
North Dakota
Bottineau
County Fair

Carrot Bars with Orange Cream Frosting

These are: bar cookies
You will need: greased and floured 9 × 13-inch pan

⅓ cup butter
¼ cup water
1 cup flour
1 cup sugar
1 teaspoon cinnamon
½ teaspoon baking soda
¼ teaspoon salt
¼ teaspoon ground nutmeg
¼ teaspoon ground ginger
1 egg, lightly beaten
¼ cup plain yogurt
½ teaspoon vanilla extract
1 cup grated carrots
⅓ cup chopped nuts
⅓ cup golden raisins

Preheat oven to 375°F.

Combine butter and water in a small saucepan. Heat until butter is melted. Remove pan from heat. In a large mixing bowl, sift together flour, sugar, cinnamon, baking soda, salt, nutmeg, and ginger. Add butter mixture, egg, yogurt, and vanilla. Stir well. Fold in carrots, nuts, and raisins. Pour into a greased and floured 9 × 13-inch pan. Bake for 20 minutes, or until a wooden toothpick inserted in center comes out clean. Let cool, then frost with Orange Cream Cheese Frosting. Cut into bars.

Orange Cream Cheese Frosting

2 tablespoons butter, at room temperature
1 3-ounce package cream cheese, at
   room temperature
½ teaspoon orange rind
1½ teaspoons orange juice
2 cups sifted confectioners' sugar, approximately

Cream together butter and cream cheese. Beat in orange rind and orange juice. Stir in enough confectioners' sugar to make a spreading consistency. Beat until light and fluffy.

Yield: about 2 dozen

Blanche Falk
Louisville,
Kentucky
Kentucky State
Fair

Carrot Cookies with Orange Butter Frosting

These are: drop cookies
You will need: greased cookie sheet

1 cup vegetable shortening
¾ cup sugar
2 eggs, lightly beaten
1 cup cooked and mashed carrots
2 cups flour
2 teaspoons baking powder
½ teaspoon salt
¾ cup shredded coconut

Preheat oven to 400°F.

Cream the shortening and sugar. Add eggs and mashed carrots. Sift together flour, baking powder, and salt. Beat into carrot mixture. Stir in shredded coconut.

Drop cookie dough by teaspoonfuls onto lightly greased cookie sheet. Leave about 2 inches between drops. Bake 8 to 10 minutes, until dough springs back when touched with finger. Let cool on wire racks before frosting.

Orange Butter Frosting

3 tablespoons butter or margarine, softened to room temperature
1½ cups confectioners' sugar
1 tablespoon orange juice
2 teaspoons grated orange peel

Cream the butter and sugar. Stir in orange juice and orange peel. Beat until frosting is smooth.

Mary H. Rusconi
Durham,
Connecticut
Durham Fair

Yield: 4 dozen

Cherry Gems

Laurel Mann has been winning blue ribbons since she first entered competition as a member of 4-H in 1969 when she was eight years old. "I always feel much more a part of the fair when I enter things," she writes, "and it's terribly exciting to attend the opening day of the fair and see what I've won."

These are: molded cookies
You will need: greased cookie sheet

½ **pound butter, softened to room temperature**
1 **cup sugar**
1 **large egg**
1½ **teaspoons vanilla extract**
2 **cups sifted flour**
½ **teaspoon baking powder**
½ **teaspoon salt**
½ **to ¾ cup chopped maraschino cherries, juice reserved for icing**
½ **cup chopped nuts or flaked coconut (optional)**

Preheat oven to 350°F.

Cream butter and sugar together. Beat in egg and vanilla until slightly foamy. Sift together flour, baking powder, and salt. Stir flour mixture and cherries alternately into creamed mixture. Mix well, but do not beat, until combined. Fold in nuts or flaked coconut.

Form into small (approximately 1-inch) balls and place 2 inches apart on a greased cookie sheet. Bake for 10 to 12 minutes. Cool on wire racks with wax paper underneath to catch drips from icing. When cookies are completely cool, ice, if desired, with the following.

Icing   **2 cups confectioners' sugar, sifted**
¼ cup liquid from maraschino cherries (or more, if needed)
½ teaspoon almond extract (rum or vanilla may be substituted)
A few drops of red food coloring (optional)

Beat all ingredients together with an electric mixer.

Yield: about 4 dozen

Laurel M. Mann
Lancaster,
California
Antelope
Valley Fair

Frosted Cashew Cookies

These are: drop cookies
You will need: ungreased cookie sheet

¼ **pound butter, softened to room temperature**
1 cup brown sugar
1 egg
⅓ **teaspoon vanilla extract**
⅓ **cup sour cream**
2 cups flour
¾ **teaspoon baking powder**
¼ **teaspoon salt**
1¾ **cups salted whole cashew nuts**

Preheat oven to 375°F.

Cream butter and sugar together until light and fluffy. Beat in egg and vanilla. Beat in sour cream. Sift together flour, baking powder, and salt and stir into liquid ingredients. Carefully fold in the cashew nuts.

Drop teaspoonfuls of cookie mixture, 2 inches apart, onto an ungreased cookie sheet. Bake for 10 minutes. Let cool on wire racks before frosting.

Frosting **4 tablespoons butter**
3 tablespoons heavy cream
¼ **teaspoon vanilla extract**
2 cups confectioners' sugar

Melt butter over medium heat and cook for a few minutes until it is lightly browned. Remove from heat and stir in cream and vanilla. Beat in sugar until frosting is light and fluffy.

Lila G. Striefel
Minot,
North Dakota
North Dakota
State Fair

Yield: 2½ dozen

Pudding Chocolate Chip Cookies

"I have always received blue ribbons on this cookie recipe," writes Alicia Thiele, who adapted it from a recipe she found in a magazine years ago. "Although everyone loves this cookie, I am always surprised at the number of people who have never had or even heard of pudding cookies."

These are: drop cookies
You will need: ungreased cookie sheet

1 cup vegetable shortening
1 cup sugar
¾ cup brown sugar
1 box (3½ ounces) instant vanilla pudding
2 eggs
2¼ cups flour
1 teaspoon baking soda
½ teaspoon salt
1 cup semisweet chocolate morsels

Preheat oven to 350°F.

Cream shortening, sugar, and brown sugar together. Stir in vanilla pudding. Beat eggs lightly and stir them into pudding mixture. Sift together flour, baking soda, and salt. Stir into pudding mixture. Blend well and fold in chocolate morsels. Drop by teaspoonfuls, 2 inches apart, onto ungreased cookie sheets and bake for 10 to 12 minutes. Cool on wire racks.

Alicia P. Thiele
Brandon,
South Dakota
Minnehaha
County Fair
and
Sioux Empire Fair

Note: For variety, substitute chocolate pudding for the vanilla.

Yield: 7 dozen

Chocolate-Coconut Bars

"I am a 4-H leader, and whenever I take these cookies to a 4-H meeting, everyone just loves them," says Adeline Oliveira.

These are: bar cookies
You will need: ungreased 9 × 13-inch baking pan

¼ pound butter
2 cups graham cracker crumbs
1 can sweetened condensed milk
3½ cups flaked coconut
1 10-ounce milk chocolate bar

Preheat oven to 350°F.

Melt the butter in a small saucepan and remove from heat. Mix graham cracker crumbs and butter in a bowl. Pat into bottom of a 9 × 13-inch baking pan. Bake for 8 minutes.

Mix condensed milk and coconut in a bowl. Spread over crust. Bake for 15 to 20 minutes more, or until lightly browned. Melt the chocolate bar in the top of a double boiler. Drizzle chocolate over top. Let cool in pan on wire rack and cut into bars.

Yield: about 2 dozen

Adeline Oliveira
Modesto,
California
Stanislaus
County Fair

Scrumptious Chocolate Layer Bars

These are: bar cookies
You will need: two greased 9 × 13-inch pans

2 cups semisweet chocolate morsels
8 ounces cream cheese
⅔ cup evaporated milk
1 cup chopped nuts
1 teaspoon vanilla extract
3 cups flour
1½ cups sugar
1 teaspoon baking powder
½ teaspoon salt
½ pound butter or margarine
2 eggs

Preheat oven to 375°F.

Combine chocolate morsels, cream cheese, and evaporated milk in a saucepan and cook over low heat, stirring constantly, until chocolate melts and mixture is smooth. Remove from heat and stir in nuts and ½ teaspoon vanilla. Blend well.

Combine remaining ingredients in a large mixer bowl. Blend with electric mixer until mixture resembles coarse crumbs. Press half of mixture into two greased 9 × 13-inch pans. Spread with the chocolate mixture. Sprinkle remaining crumbs over chocolate mixture and bake for 35 to 40 minutes, or until golden brown. Let cool in pans on racks, then cut into bars.

Mrs. Merle
Mishler
Hollsopple,
Pennsylvania
Somerset
County Fair

Yield: about 100

Chocolate Marshmallow Drops

These are: drop cookies
You will need: greased cookie sheet

½ **cup vegetable shortening**
1 **cup sugar**
1 **egg**
1 **teaspoon vanilla extract**
½ **cup milk**
1¾ **cups sifted flour**
½ **teaspoon baking soda**
½ **teaspoon salt**
½ **cup cocoa**
½ **cup chopped nuts**
½ **cup chopped maraschino cherries**
60 **or more small marshmallows**
Milk Chocolate Frosting (page 125)

Preheat oven to 350°F.

Cream together shortening and sugar until light and fluffy. Beat in egg, vanilla, and milk. Sift together flour, baking soda, salt, and cocoa. Stir into creamed mixture. Stir in nuts and cherries. Drop by teaspoonfuls onto greased cookie sheet, leaving 2 inches between cookies. Bake for 8 minutes. Remove from oven and press a marshmallow into each cookie. Return to oven until marshmallows start to soften, about 1½ minutes. Cool on wire racks. Spread with chocolate frosting, if desired.

Yield: about 60

Connie Price
Portland, Indiana
Jay County Fair

Chocolate Chip Cookies (That Taste Like Candy)

"Folks have been making chocolate chip cookies for years and entering them in local and state fairs," writes Ellen Lelasher. "The recipe is basic but my mother always told me 'Judges love nuts.' The first time I made the cookies and entered them in the North Haven Fair, I won first prize. Don't be afraid to add more nuts and chocolate pieces."

These are: drop cookies
You will need: ungreased cookie sheet

2¼ cups flour
1 teaspoon baking soda
1 teaspoon salt
1 pound butter, softened to room temperature
¾ cup sugar
¾ cup brown sugar
1 teaspoon vanilla extract
½ teaspoon water
2 eggs
2 12-ounce packages semisweet chocolate chips
1 pound nuts, coarsely chopped

Preheat oven to 375°F.

Sift together flour, baking soda, and salt. Set aside. Cream together butter and sugars until light and fluffy. Beat in vanilla, water, and eggs. Combine with flour and mix well. Fold in chocolate chips and nuts. Drop by teaspoonfuls, 2 inches apart, onto ungreased cookie sheets. Bake for 8 to 10 minutes. Cool on wire racks.

Ellen A. Lelasher
Northford,
Connecticut
North Haven Fair

Yield: 50 to 60

Chocolate Chip Cookies II

Samantha is a nine-year-old fourth grader from Sterling Junction, Massachusetts. She writes that she and her mother "take time at least once a week to do some cooking and baking together. My mom says that these are some of the things I need to know 'for life'. . . . My specialty is cookies. I was encouraged by my family to enter my chocolate chip cookie recipe in the junior category at the Sterling Town Fair. I took first place for this recipe, which is my adaptation of the one found on the back of Hershey's Chocolate Chips. This recipe makes a soft cookie, which is just the way I like it."

These are: drop cookies
You will need: ungreased cookie sheet

½ pound butter, softened to room temperature
¾ cup sugar
¾ cup light brown sugar
2 jumbo eggs
1½ teaspoons vanilla extract
2¼ cups flour
1 teaspoon baking soda
½ teaspoon salt
2 cups semisweet chocolate chips

Preheat oven to 375°F.
　　Cream together butter and both sugars until light and fluffy. Beat in eggs, one at a time, then vanilla. Sift together flour, baking soda, and salt and stir into creamed mixture. Fold in chocolate chips.

Drop by teaspoonfuls onto ungreased cookie sheet. Bake for about 8 minutes, or until lightly browned around the edges and centers of cookies look firm but are still soft. Remove from oven and leave cookies on sheet for about 10 minutes. Remove with a spatula, eat and enjoy.

Yield: 90 to 100

Samantha
McQuain
Sterling Junction,
Massachusetts
Sterling Town Fair

Chocolate Chunk Cookies

"When I was in school, I could never make a decent 'Toll House' chocolate chip cookie," writes Karen Keller-Sherman. "So for many years I've been trying different cookie recipes. This prizewinning recipe is the result of all my many years of experimentation."

These are: drop cookies
You will need: cookie sheet lined with baking parchment

1 pound butter, softened to room temperature
2 cups dark brown sugar
3 eggs, beaten
1 tablespoon vanilla extract
5 cups flour
1 teaspoon salt (optional)
1 teaspoon baking soda
1 cup rolled oats
4 8-ounce bars of semisweet chocolate, broken into large ½-inch chunks
2 cups unsalted chopped macadamia nuts (optional)
   or
2 cups flaked coconut (optional)
   or
2 cups raisins (optional)

Preheat oven to 350°F.
   Cream together the butter and sugar until very light and fluffy. Beat in eggs and vanilla. Sift together the flour, salt, and baking soda. Add to the creamed mixture, alternating with rolled oats. Beat 3 to 4 minutes. Mixture will be dry. Stir in the chocolate chunks (and nuts or other ingredients, if

you choose to use them). The best way to mix everything is to use your hands. Cover a cookie sheet with baking parchment. Use a #20 ice cream scoop or drop by tablespoonfuls onto cookie sheet 3 to 4 inches apart.

Bake for 8 to 11 minutes, depending on your oven. Pull them out of the oven while they are still light in color and soft. Let rest on cookie sheet 30 seconds, then remove to a wire rack to cool. Store these cookies in an airtight container with a slice of apple or bread to keep them soft.

Note: These cookies freeze very well. When frozen, just cook in the microwave for 30 to 60 seconds. They'll taste as if they just came out of the oven.

Yield: 4 dozen

Karen Keller-
Sherman
Castro Valley,
California
Alameda
County Fair

Chocolate Cookies

These are: molded cookies
You will need: greased cookie sheet

2 ounces (2 squares) unsweetened chocolate
½ cup vegetable shortening
2 cups sugar
2 teaspoons vanilla extract
2 eggs
2 cups flour
2 teaspoons baking powder
½ teaspoon salt
⅓ cup milk
½ cup chopped nuts
½ cup confectioners' sugar

Melt the chocolate squares in the top of a double boiler. Cream together shortening, sugar, and vanilla. Beat in eggs and chocolate. Sift flour, baking powder, and salt together. Stir into chocolate mixture, alternating with the milk. Blend well and fold in the nuts. Cover and chill in refrigerator for 2 to 3 hours.

Preheat oven to 350°F.

Form into balls 1 inch in diameter. Roll in confectioners' sugar and place on a greased cookie sheet, leaving 2 to 3 inches between each one. Bake for about 20 minutes. Cool on wire racks.

Yield: about 5 dozen

Margaret Long
Huron, South
Dakota
South Dakota
State Fair

42

Chocolate Crackles

These are: molded cookies
You will need: greased cookie sheet

2 squares (2 ounces) unsweetened chocolate
¼ cup vegetable oil
1 cup sugar
2 eggs
1 teaspoon vanilla extract
1 cup flour
1 teaspoon baking powder
½ teaspoon salt
½ cup chopped nuts (optional)
Confectioners' sugar

Melt the chocolate in the top of a double boiler. Remove to a mixing bowl and blend with vegetable oil, sugar, eggs, and vanilla. Beat well until mixture is smooth. Sift together flour, baking powder, and salt. Stir into liquid ingredients. Fold in nuts, if using. Chill dough in refrigerator for several hours.

Preheat oven to 350°F.

Form dough into 1-inch balls, roll in confectioners' sugar, and place 2 inches apart on a lightly greased cookie sheet. Bake for 10 minutes. Cool on wire racks.

Yield: about 40 cookies

Edna Sherman
Sioux Falls,
South Dakota
Sioux Empire Fair

Chocolate Fudge Cookies

"My cookie recipe was an accident almost from beginning to end," writes Carolyn Austin. "The day before cookie entries were due I was experimenting. The first dough I made was too gooey. I refrigerated the dough, but in my baking frenzy I chilled it too long. I set it out on the counter and continued my other baking. Later I noticed my son, Scott, eating the raw dough. He said it was delicious. I dipped out walnut-size balls and baked those. They weren't attractive enough so the next batch I rolled the balls in granulated sugar. WAH LAH! Out of the whole recipe, the morning of the fair I had only five cookies left! My husband and sons kept snitching them, saying, 'just one more, she'll never know.'"

These are: molded cookies
You will need: greased cookie sheet

3 squares (3 ounces) unsweetened chocolate
¼ pound butter, softened to room temperature
½ cup butter-flavored vegetable shortening
1 cup brown sugar
½ cup granulated sugar, plus additional sugar
**   for coating**
2 eggs
½ teaspoon vanilla extract
2¼ cups flour
1 teaspoon salt
1 teaspoon baking soda

Melt the chocolate in the top of a double boiler and let cool. Cream together butter, shortening, and both sugars until fluffy. Beat in eggs, one at a time, then vanilla extract. Beat in melted chocolate. Sift together flour, salt, and baking soda. Stir into creamed mixture. Cover and chill (about 2 hours).

Preheat oven to 375°F.

Make walnut-size balls and roll in granulated sugar. Place 2 inches apart on a lightly greased cookie sheet. Bake for 9½ minutes. Cookies will look gooey when taken from oven. Allow to cool just slightly and remove to wire rack to cool completely. The outside will be crisp and the inside should remain soft.

Yield: about 4 dozen

Carolyn T. Austin
Nashville,
Tennessee
Tennessee State
Fair

Chocolate Pixies

These are: molded cookies
You will need: greased cookie sheet

2 cups sifted flour
2 teaspoons baking powder
½ teaspoon salt
4 tablespoons butter
4 squares (4 ounces) unsweetened chocolate
2 cups sugar
4 eggs
½ cup chopped walnuts
Confectioners' sugar

Preheat oven to 300°F.

Sift together flour, baking powder, and salt. Set aside. Combine butter and chocolate in a heavy saucepan or in the top of a double boiler and melt over low heat. Remove from heat and let cool slightly. Beat in the sugar and, when mixture is smooth, continue beating in the eggs, one at a time. Beat until mixture is smooth and fluffy. Stir in flour mixture and blend in walnuts. Chill in refrigerator for at least 15 minutes.

Roll into balls using 1 tablespoon of dough for each ball. Roll in confectioners' sugar and place 2 inches apart on a greased cookie sheet. Bake for 18 to 20 minutes. Cool on wire racks.

Yield: 3 dozen

Marge Stinnett
Fresno, California
Fresno Fair

Cloverleaf Cookies

These are: molded cookies
You will need: ungreased cookie sheet

¾ cup brown sugar
½ cup white sugar
½ pound butter or margarine, softened to
    room temperature
1 egg
2 teaspoons vanilla extract
2 cups flour
1 teaspoon baking soda
¾ teaspoon salt
½ cup mini-chocolate chips
¼ cup chunky peanut butter
1 square (1 ounce) unsweetened chocolate,
    melted and cooled

Cream together both sugars and butter until light and fluffy. Beat in egg and vanilla extract. Sift together flour, baking soda, and salt. Stir flour into creamed mixture. Divide dough into three parts and place each in a small bowl. Fold chocolate chips into one portion of dough. Fold peanut butter into second portion of dough. Fold melted chocolate into third portion of dough. Refrigerate all dough for ½ hour for easier handling.

Preheat oven to 375°F.

Shape ½ teaspoon of each dough into a ball. Place three balls, one of each flavor, in a cloverleaf shape on an ungreased cookie sheet. Leave about 2 inches between each cloverleaf. Bake for 10 to 12 minutes, until set. Let cool on cookie sheets for 1 minute. Remove carefully with a spatula and cool on wire racks.

Patricia Ewald
Wausau, Wisconsin
Wisconsin
Valley Fair

Yield: 3½ dozen

47

Coconut Clouds

Laura Case York has won prizes in several state fairs. She writes, "State fairs may differ somewhat, but one fact holds true for all—use the best ingredients you can, because the judges will know!"

These are: drop cookies
You will need: cookie sheet lined with baking parchment

2 egg whites, at room temperature
½ teaspoon vanilla extract
¼ teaspoon salt
⅔ cup sugar
1⅓ cups flaked coconut (1 3-ounce can)

Preheat oven to 325°F.

Beat egg whites, vanilla, and salt until soft peaks form. Gradually add sugar, beating until stiff peaks form. Fold in coconut. Drop by teaspoonfuls 1½ inches apart onto a cookie sheet lined with baking parchment. Bake for 20 minutes. Cool on parchment paper.

Yield: 2 dozen

Laura Case York
Valrico, Florida
Florida State Fair

Cracker Jack Cookies

These cookies made from an old family recipe are excellent tucked into a lunch box.

These are: drop cookies
You will need: ungreased cookie sheet

1 cup vegetable shortening
1 cup brown sugar
1 cup sugar
2 eggs
2 teaspoons vanilla extract
1½ cups flour
1 teaspoon baking powder
1 teaspoon baking soda
2 cups rolled oats
1 cup flaked coconut
2 cups Rice Crispies

Preheat oven to 350°F.

Cream shortening together with both sugars. Beat in eggs and add vanilla. Sift together flour, baking powder, and baking soda and mix with shortening and egg mixture. Stir in rolled oats and coconut, then fold in Rice Crispies. Drop by teaspoonfuls, 2 inches apart, onto an ungreased cookie sheet. Bake for 10 to 12 minutes. Cool on wire racks.

Yield: about 5 dozen

Edna Sherman
Sioux Falls,
South Dakota
Sioux Empire Fair

Cream Wafers

These are: rolled cookies with sandwich filling
You will need: ungreased cookie sheet

½ pound butter, softened to room temperature
⅓ cup heavy cream
2 cups flour
Granulated sugar

Cream the butter until light and fluffy. Beat in cream and stir in flour. Mix thoroughly and chill for 1 hour in refrigerator.

Preheat oven to 375°F.

Roll dough out to ⅛-inch thickness on a lightly floured surface. Cut into 1 ½-inch rounds. Dip in granulated sugar, turning to coat both sides. Place on ungreased cookie sheet, leaving 1 inch space between cookies. Prick each cookie in 4 places with a fork. Bake for 7 to 9 minutes, or until slightly puffy. Cool on wire racks. Prepare filling.

Creamy Butter Filling

4 tablespoons butter, softened to room temperature
¾ cup sifted confectioners' sugar
1 teaspoon vanilla extract

Blend butter with confectioners' sugar and vanilla. Put two cooled cookies together with filling.

Yield: about 2 dozen

Adeline Oliveira
Modesto,
California
Stanislaus
County Fair

Currant Ginger Cookies

These are: drop cookies
You will need: greased cookie sheet

¾ cup vegetable shortening
⅔ cup sugar
1 egg
¼ cup molasses
2¼ cups sifted flour
2 teaspoons baking soda
1 teaspoon salt
1 teaspoon ground ginger
½ teaspoon cinnamon
¼ teaspoon ground cloves
1½ cups zante currants
Additional sugar for coating

Cream together shortening and sugar. Beat in egg and molasses. Sift together flour, baking soda, salt, ginger, cinnamon, and cloves and add to creamed mixture. Stir in currants and mix well. Chill dough for 30 minutes.

Preheat oven to 375°F.

Drop by teaspoonfuls into granulated sugar and roll into balls. Place on lightly greased cookie sheets 2 inches apart. Bake for 8 to 10 minutes. Cool on wire racks.

Yield: 3 dozen

Ursula Maurer
Wauwatosa,
Wisconsin
Wisconsin State
Fair

Date Bars I

"I have worked twenty-five years for the State of Oregon, Department of Transportation, as an office manager," says Fran Neavoll. In my spare time, I practice baking cookies all year long. I taste to determine if it is an absolutely perfect cookie and then give the extras to the local needy lunch program. I am a perfectionist and it is a challenge to compete with Oregon's finest cooks. My goal was to win the 'best cookie' award at the State Fair. That dream came true in 1986."

These are: bar cookies
You will need: greased 8-inch square pan

2½ cups chopped dates
1 cup water
¼ pound butter
½ cup honey
½ teaspoon vanilla extract
1¼ cups rolled oats
1½ cups whole wheat flour
½ teaspoon baking soda
¼ teaspoon salt
⅔ cups chopped walnuts

Combine dates and water and simmer, stirring frequently, until mixture thickens (7 to 10 minutes). Remove from heat and let cool.

Preheat oven to 350°F.

Cream together butter, honey, and vanilla extract until mixture is light and fluffy. In a separate bowl, combine rolled oats, flour, baking soda, salt, and walnuts. Mix well, then stir into creamed mixture.

Press half of the honey-flour mixture into a greased 8-inch square pan. Cover with date filling and crumble remaining honey-flour mixture over the top. Press the honey-flour mixture down slightly with your hands. Bake for 30 minutes. Cut into bars when cool.

Yield: about 20

Fran Neavoll
Salem, Oregon
Oregon State Fair

Date Bars II

"This recipe belonged to my grandmother, who passed away a few years ago at the age of 99," writes Marcia Wolff. "My mother and I figured the recipe to be nearly seventy-five years old. It's an easy, delicious recipe, especially when made with butter."

These are: bar cookies
You will need: greased 9 × 13-inch pan

¾ cup sugar
1 cup water
1¼ cups dates, chopped
1¾ cups quick-cooking oats
1½ cups flour
1 teaspoon baking soda
½ teaspoon salt
1 cup brown sugar
¼ pound plus 4 tablespoons butter or margarine, softened to room temperature

Combine sugar, water, and dates in a saucepan and simmer until thick and spreadable (7 to 10 minutes).
Preheat oven to 350°F.
In a large mixing bowl, combine oats, flour, baking soda, salt, and brown sugar and mix well. Cut in butter as for a pie crust (but mixture does not have to hold together). Spread half the mixture in a greased 9 × 13-inch pan. Spread date mixture evenly over top, then sprinkle with remaining oatmeal mixture. Pat down entire surface. Bake for 30 minutes. Cool in pan on wire rack. Cut into bars.

Marcia Wolff
La Porte, Indiana
La Porte
County Fair

Yield: about 4 dozen

Date Cookies

These are: refrigerator cookies
You will need: greased cookie sheet

½ **pound dates, chopped**
⅓ **cup water**
½ **cup nuts, chopped fine**
¼ **pound butter or margarine**
½ **cup brown sugar**
½ **cup granulated sugar**
1 **egg**
2 **cups flour**
½ **teaspoon baking soda**

Simmer the dates in ⅓ cup water until soft (7 to 10 minutes). Remove from heat and add the nuts. Reserve.

Cream butter and sugars until light and fluffy. Beat in the egg. Sift flour and baking soda and stir into creamed mixture to make a soft dough. Divide dough into two equal portions. Sprinkle flour on two large pieces of wax paper. Press dough out with hands on paper to make two rectangles. Spread date mixture on top of each rectangle. Roll into jelly rolls and wrap in wax paper. Cool in refrigerator until dough is firm.

Preheat oven to 375°F.

Slice dough ½ inch thick and bake on greased cookie sheets for 12 to 15 minutes.

Yield: about 6 dozen

Elizabeth Anderson
Winston-Salem,
North Carolina
Dixie Classic Fair

Date Orange Bars

These are: bar cookies
You will need: greased 11 × 7 × 1½-inch pan

4 tablespoons butter or margarine, softened
    to room temperature
½ cup brown sugar
1 egg
1 teaspoon grated orange peel
1 cup sifted flour
½ teaspoon baking powder
½ teaspoon baking soda
¼ cup milk
¼ cup orange juice
¾ cup chopped walnuts
½ cup snipped pitted dates
Confectioners' sugar for topping

Preheat oven to 350°F.

Cream butter and sugar until fluffy. Beat in egg and orange peel. Sift together flour, baking powder, and baking soda. Add flour to creamed mixture. Stir in milk, orange juice, walnuts, and dates. Spread in a greased 11 × 7 × 1 ½-inch pan. Bake for 25 minutes. Cool in pan on wire rack, sprinkle with confectioners' sugar, and cut into bars.

Yield: about 6 dozen

Christine C. Kirk
Merced, California
Merced
County Fair

Divinity Surprise Cookies

These are: drop cookies
You will need: cookie sheet lined with baking parchment

3 egg whites, at room temperature
1 cup sugar
1 teaspoon vanilla extract
1 12-ounce package chocolate chips

Preheat oven to 300°F.

Beat egg whites until stiff. Continue beating and gradually add sugar. Fold in vanilla extract and chocolate chips. Drop by teaspoonfuls, 2 inches apart, onto cookie sheet lined with baking parchment. Bake for 30 minutes. Let cool on parchment.

Yield: about 4 dozen

Alice Holtin
Muscle Shoals
North Alabama
State Fair

Filled Cookies

These are: molded cookies
You will need: greased miniature muffin tins

3 ounces cream cheese
¼ pound butter or margarine
1 cup flour
¾ cup brown sugar
1 egg
1 tablespoon margarine
1 teaspoon vanilla extract
1 cup chopped pecans

Preheat oven to 350°F.

Cut the cream cheese and butter into the flour until mixture just holds together. Divide into 24 small balls and press into well-greased miniature muffin tins.

Mix together the remaining ingredients. Press a small amount into the center of each cookie. Bake for 15 to 20 minutes, or until lightly brown.

Yield: 2 dozen

Margie Wagner
Mount Sterling,
Illinois
Brown
County Fair
Schuyler
Rushville Fair

Forgotten Cookies

Put these in the oven, turn it off, and forget them.

These are: drop cookies
You will need: cookie sheet lined with baking parchment

2 egg whites, at room temperature
¾ cup sugar
1 16-ounce package chocolate bits

Preheat oven to 375°F.

Beat egg whites until stiff. Beat sugar in gradually until completely incorporated. Fold in chocolate bits. Drop by teaspoonfuls on a cookie sheet lined with baking parchment, spacing cookies 2 inches apart. Place in oven, turn off oven, and leave until completely cool.

Yield: about 2 dozen

Leota Shaneyfelt
Portland, Indiana
Jay County Fair

Country Ginger Raisin Cookies

These are: molded cookies
You will need: greased cookie sheet

¼ pound plus 4 tablespoons butter, softened to
    room temperature
1 cup sugar
1 egg
¼ cup molasses
2¼ cups flour
2 teaspoons baking soda
½ teaspoon salt
2 teaspoons ground ginger
½ teaspoon cinnamon
¼ teaspoon ground cloves
1½ cup raisins
Additional granulated sugar for coating

Cream together the butter and sugar until light and
fluffy. Beat in egg and molasses. Sift together flour,
baking soda, salt, ginger, cinnamon, and cloves. Stir
into creamed mixture. Stir in raisins and mix well.
Chill cookie mixture for 1 hour or longer.

    Preheat oven to 375°F.

    Shape cookie dough into 1-inch balls and roll in
granulated sugar. Place 2 inches apart on a greased
cookie sheet. Bake for 10 minutes.

Yield: about 4 dozen

Doris Swank
Naples, Florida
Collier County Fair

Gumdrop Cookies

Children will love these. Make them for birthday parties or other special occasions.

These are: drop cookies
You will need: ungreased cookie sheet

1 cup shortening
1 cup brown sugar
1 cup granulated sugar
2 eggs
1 teaspoon vanilla extract
2 cups flour
½ teaspoon salt
1 teaspoon baking soda
1 teaspoon baking powder
2 cups rolled oats
1 cup gumdrops, cut into small pieces
1 cup coconut flakes

Preheat oven to 350°F.

Cream shortening and sugars together. Add eggs and vanilla and beat well. Sift together flour, salt, baking soda, and baking powder. Stir into creamed mixture. Stir in rolled oats. Fold in gumdrops and coconut flakes. Drop by teaspoonfuls, 2 inches apart, on ungreased cookie sheets. Bake for about 12 minutes, or until cookies are browned. Cool on wire racks.

Yield: about 6 dozen

Mrs. Eldon
Wichmann
St. Libory,
Nebraska
Howard
County Fair

High Fiber, Low Sugar Oatmeal Chews

"I concocted this recipe through trial and error to compete in a new category of High Fiber–Low Sugar Cookie at the 1986 Wisconsin State Fair," writes Ursula Maurer. "I wanted a cookie that was moist and tasty yet as high in fiber as possible. It was a challenge to me because I love healthful baked goods with lots of texture."

These are: drop cookies
You will need: greased cookie sheet

½ cup raisins
1 cup water
1½ cups whole wheat flour
½ teaspoon baking soda
½ teaspoon salt
1 teaspoon cinnamon
1 tablespoon buttermilk powder, available in
  health food stores
1 tablespoon millers' bran (unprocessed bran)
1¾ cups rolled oats
½ cup sunflower seeds (unsalted, raw or roasted)
½ cup chopped nuts
½ cup prunes or apricots, diced
1 egg
⅓ cup safflower oil
½ cup honey

Preheat oven to 350°F.

Simmer raisins in 1 cup water for 5 minutes to plump them. Drain, reserving ¼ cup of the liquid.

Mix whole wheat flour, baking soda, salt, cinnamon, buttermilk powder, and bran. Add oats, sunflower seeds, nuts, and prunes or apricots. Mix again.

Beat together the egg, reserved ¼ cup raisin water, safflower oil, and honey. Stir liquid mixture into the dry ingredients. Mix well. Drop by teaspoonfuls onto greased cookie sheets about 2 inches apart. Bake for 15 minutes, or until slightly brown around the edges. Cool on wire racks.

Yield: 2 to 3 dozen

Ursula Maurer
Wauwatosa,
Wisconsin
Wisconsin State
Fair

Honey Crinkle Cookies

"I love to bake and I enter four or five items in the fair each year," says Patricia Semrick. "I come from a family that loves to eat. My mother always planned dessert before dinner. My father ran a candy and ice cream store and made his own."

These are: drop cookies
You will need: ungreased cookie sheet

⅔ **cup vegetable oil**
1 **cup sugar**
1 **egg**
½ **teaspoon vanilla extract**
¼ **cup honey**
2 **cups flour**
2 **teaspoons baking soda**
¾ **teaspoon mace**
½ **teaspoon salt**
Additional granulated sugar for coating

Preheat oven to 350°F.

Combine vegetable oil and sugar and beat well. Beat in egg, vanilla, and honey. Sift together flour, baking soda, mace, and salt. Stir flour mixture into liquid ingredients and mix well to blend. Drop by teaspoonfuls into granulated sugar and roll into balls. Place 2 inches apart on an ungreased cookie sheet. Bake for 12 to 15 minutes. Let stand for a minute or so before removing from pan. Cool on wire racks.

Yield: 2½ dozen

Patricia A. Semrick
Fresno, California
Fresno County Fair

Honey Nut Bars

These are: bar cookies
You will need: ungreased 9-inch square pan

1¼ cups flour
⅓ cup sugar
¼ pound butter
1 cup chopped pecans
1 cup brown sugar, packed
¼ pound butter, melted
2 eggs
2 tablespoons honey

Preheat oven to 350°F.

Blend flour, sugar, and butter together until mixture is crumbly. Add ¼ cup pecans and reserve the rest. Press mixture into an ungreased 9-inch square pan. Bake for 15 minutes, or until edges are lightly browned. Meanwhile, combine brown sugar, remaining pecans, melted butter, eggs, and honey and mix well. Pour over hot cookie crust and return to oven for 25 minutes, or until a toothpick comes out clean and dry. Let cool in pan on wire rack and cut into bars.

Yield: about 16

Doris Swank
Naples, Florida
Collier County Fair

Hungarian Butter Horns

Judy Bihn found this recipe in a church cookbook, made some changes to suit her family's tastes, and won first place at the Arizona State Fair.

These are: rolled and filled cookies
You will need: greased cookie sheet

4 cups flour
½ teaspoon salt
1 tablespoon dry yeast
½ pound plus 4 tablespoons butter
3 egg yolks
½ cup sour cream
1 teaspoon vanilla extract

Filling   **3 egg whites**
1 cup sugar
¾ cup finely chopped nuts
½ cup finely chopped dried apricots
½ cup finely chopped pitted prunes
1 teaspoon vanilla extract

Confectioners' sugar for dusting

Sift flour and salt into a large mixing bowl. Stir in yeast. Cut in butter and mix as for pie crust, until mixture resembles coarse meal. In a separate bowl, beat the egg yolks together with sour cream and vanilla. Stir into flour mixture to make a stiff dough. Cover and refrigerate while you prepare the filling.
   Mix all filling ingredients together. Reserve.
   Preheat oven to 350°F.

Divide the dough into 8 parts. Roll each part into a circle and cut each circle into 8 wedge-shaped pieces. (Ms. Bihn rolls out dough between two sheets of wax paper.) Spread 1 teaspoon of filling on each wedge. Roll each wedge, starting from the wide end into the center, and shape like crescents. Place on a lightly greased cookie sheet and bake for about 20 minutes. Dough will rise as the cookies bake. Cool on wire racks and dust with confectioners' sugar.

Yield: 64

Judy Bihn
Phoenix, Arizona
Arizona State Fair

Ice Box Cookies

These are: refrigerator cookies
You will need: greased cookie sheet

½ pound butter, softened to room temperature
2 cups brown sugar
2 eggs
3½ cups flour
½ teaspoon salt
1 teaspoon baking soda
½ teaspoon cinnamon
1 cup chopped nuts

Cream butter and sugar together. Beat eggs lightly and beat into butter mixture. Sift together the flour, salt, baking soda, and cinnamon. Stir into the wet ingredients and mix well. Fold in the nuts.

Divide dough into 4 equal parts and roll into logs approximately 1 inch in diameter. Wrap in plastic and refrigerate for several hours or overnight. May be frozen until ready to use.

Preheat oven to 400°F.

Slice cookie logs into rounds approximately ⅛ inch thick and place on greased cookie sheets, leaving 1 inch between each cookie. Bake for about 10 minutes, or until golden. Cool on wire racks.

Yield: about 6 ½ dozen

Beth Raptis
Orangeburg,
South Carolina
Orangeburg
County Fair

Italian Sesame Sticks

These are molded cookies
You will need: foil-lined cookie sheet

4 cups flour
1 tablespoon plus 1 teaspoon baking powder
½ teaspoon salt
½ pound butter or margarine, softened
1 teaspoon vanilla extract
1 cup sugar
3 eggs
1 cup milk
2 cups sesame seeds

Sift together flour, baking powder, and salt and set aside. In the large bowl of an electric mixer, cream the butter. Beat in vanilla and sugar until fluffy. Add eggs one at a time, beating well after each. Gradually mix in flour at low speed, just until smooth. Chill dough in refrigerator for about 20 minutes.

Preheat oven to 350°F.

Pour milk into a soup bowl and spread sesame seeds on wax paper. Shape about ¼ cup of dough at a time on a lightly floured board into a 10-inch rope that is ½ inch in diameter. Cut ropes into 2-inch lengths. Handle gently as the dough is delicate. Dip each piece in milk then roll in sesame seeds. Place 1 inch apart on foil-lined cookie sheets. Bake for 20 to 22 minutes, or until golden brown. Cool on wire racks.

Yield: about 8 dozen

Cindee Tine
Middletown,
Connecticut
Durham Fair

Italian Wedding Cookies

These are: molded cookies
You will need: ungreased cookie sheet

7 large eggs
1 cup sugar
1 cup vegetable oil
1 teaspoon anise extract
4½ cups flour
2 heaping tablespoons baking powder

Topping   2 cups confectioners' sugar, sifted
2 to 3 tablespoons water
1 tablespoon anise extract
Colored sugar or colored nonpareils

Beat the eggs until light and fluffy, then beat in sugar until smooth. Beat in vegetable oil and anise extract. Sift together flour and baking powder. Stir into liquid ingredients and mix well. Chill in refrigerator for 20 minutes.

Preheat oven to 400°F.

Roll into 1-inch balls and bake on ungreased cookie sheet for about 10 minutes, until cookies are lightly browned. Cool on wire racks with sheets of wax paper underneath.

Mix together the confectioners' sugar, water, and anise extract to make a thin icing. Dip cool cookies into icing, then sprinkle with colored sugar or nonpareils.

Yield: about 5 dozen

Marion Flynn
West Falmouth,
Massachusetts
Barnstable
County Fair

Lemon Bars

Linda Gustafson submits about twenty-five baking entries to the Kane County Fair in Illinois every year, competing directly with her daughter and son-in-law. The following lemon bars are among her most popular recipes.

These are: bar cookies
You will need: 8½ × 13-inch pan or 9 × 12-inch pan

Crust   ½ **pound margarine**
2 cups flour
¼ **teaspoon salt**
½ **cup sugar**

Preheat oven to 350°F.

Blend all crust ingredients until mixture is the consistency of coarse cornmeal. (This can be done in a food processor.) Press into an 8½ × 13-inch pan (or 9 × 12-inch pan). Bake for 20 minutes, or until golden; meanwhile, prepare the filling.

Filling   **4 eggs**
2 cups sugar
4 tablespoons flour
½ **teaspoon baking powder**
7 tablespoons lemon juice
1 teaspoon grated lemon rind
Confectioners' sugar

Beat the eggs until they are light and thick. Gradually beat in the sugar, flour, baking powder, lemon juice, and lemon rind. Remove the crust from oven and pour filling evenly across the top. Return to oven and bake 20 minutes longer, or until top is golden and filling is set. Let cool in pan on wire rack. Sprinkle with confectioners' sugar and cut into squares.

Yield: about 30

Linda Gustafson
Batavia, Illinois
Kane County Fair

Lemon Cookie Sandwiches

Laura Case York is employed as a television meteorologist and baking has always been one of her favorite hobbies. Her Lemon Cookie Sandwiches won the Cookie Sweepstakes at the Kentucky State Fair. Her television station printed the recipe and made it available to interested viewers. They mailed out more than fifteen hundred copies. In 1984 she married and moved to Florida, where she won the Cookie Sweepstakes at the Florida State Fair.

These are: refrigerator cookies with sandwich filling
You will need: ungreased cookie sheet

½ cup sugar
¼ pound butter or margarine, at
    room temperature
2 egg yolks
1 tablespoon water
1 teaspoon vanilla extract
1½ cups flour
½ teaspoon salt
¼ teaspoon baking soda

Lemon Filling   1 cup confectioners' sugar
2 teaspoons butter or margarine, at
    room temperature
1 teaspoon grated lemon peel
1 tablespoon plus 1½ teaspoons lemon juice

2 egg whites
⅔ cup finely chopped nuts

Cream together sugar and butter. Beat in egg yolks, water and vanilla. Sift together flour, salt, and baking soda. Stir into creamed mixture. Divide dough in half; shape each half into a log approximately 7 inches long and 1½ inches in diameter. Wrap in plastic and refrigerate until firm, about 4 hours.

Meanwhile, mix all filling ingredients until smooth.

Preheat oven to 400°F.

Cut logs into ⅛-inch slices. Place 1 inch apart on ungreased cookie sheet. Beat egg whites slightly; stir in nuts. Spoon ½ teaspoon of the nut mixture onto half of the dough slices, leaving remaining slices plain. Bake for about 6 minutes, until edges begin to brown. Remove from baking sheet and cool on wire racks. Make sandwiches with Lemon Filling, using nut-topped cookies for tops.

Yield: about 4 dozen

Laura Case York
Valrico, Florida
Florida State Fair

Marshmallow Fudge Bars

These are: bar cookies
You will need: greased 9 × 13-inch baking pan

1½ cups sugar
½ cup vegetable shortening
3 eggs
1 teaspoon vanilla extract
1½ cups flour
½ teaspoon baking soda
¼ cup cocoa
½ teaspoon salt
¾ cup chopped nuts
Marshmallows

Preheat oven to 350°F.

Cream together sugar and shortening. Beat in eggs, one at a time, then vanilla. Sift together flour, baking soda, cocoa, and salt. Stir into creamed mixture and fold in the nuts.

Pour into a greased 9 × 13-inch baking pan and bake for 20 minutes. Remove and place marshmallows 2 inches apart all across the top. Return to oven just until marshmallows melt. Let cool in pan on rack. Prepare frosting:

Frosting ½ cup brown sugar
¼ cup water
3 tablespoons cocoa
3 tablespoons butter
1 teaspoon vanilla extract
1½ cups confectioners' sugar

Combine sugar, water, and cocoa in a saucepan and bring to a boil. Remove from heat and stir in butter and vanilla. Beat in the confectioners' sugar. Spread over melted marshmallows. Let cool and cut into squares or rectangles.

Yield: about 4 dozen

Mrs. Eldon
Wichmann
St. Libory,
Nebraska
Howard
County Fair

Minnie's Pfeffernusse Cookies

Michele Glazier inherited the recipe for these cookies from her grandmother. It has been a long-time family favorite and a favorite with judges as well.

These are: molded cookies
You will need: ungreased cookie sheet

½ cup vegetable shortening
¼ pound butter or margarine
1 cup granulated sugar
1 cup brown sugar
1 cup honey
2 eggs
1 cup black coffee (drinking temperature—not too hot)
1 teaspoon nutmeg
1 teaspoon ground cloves
1 teaspoon cinnamon
1½ teaspoons aniseed
7 cups flour
3 teaspoons baking soda

Cream together shortening, butter, and both sugars. Beat in honey and eggs. Beat in coffee. Stir in all the spices. Sift together flour and baking soda. Stir into liquid ingredients. This will make a soft, sticky dough. Cover and refrigerate overnight.

Preheat oven to 375°F.

Shape into balls the size of a walnut. Bake on ungreased cookie sheets for about 15 minutes, or until cookies are golden brown and spring back when touched. Cool slightly and roll cookies in confectioners' sugar.

Yield: a large batch (about 300 cookies)

Michele Glazier
Kalispell, Montana
Northwest
Montana Fair

Drop Molasses Cookies

These are: drop cookies
You will need: greased cookie sheet

¼ pound plus 4 tablespoons butter
1 cup sugar
4 tablespoons molasses
1 egg
2 cups flour
2 teaspoons baking powder
1 teaspoon cinnamon
1 teaspoon ground cloves
½ teaspoon ground ginger
Additional sugar for coating

Preheat oven to 375°F.

Cream together butter and 1 cup sugar. Add molasses and egg and beat well. Sift together the flour, baking powder, cinnamon, cloves, and ginger and add to butter mixture. Stir until well mixed. Roll into small balls, no bigger than walnuts, dip each ball in sugar, and place 2 inches apart on a greased cookie sheet. Bake 15 to 18 minutes. Cool on wire racks.

Yield: 2½ dozen

Mary Harmon
Empire, California
Stanislaus
County Fair

Rolled Molasses Cookies

The recipe for these cookies has been handed down in Elizabeth Burgett's family for four generations, and since her daughter and granddaughter also make it, the recipe is six generations old. "The last cookie is always as good as the first one," she writes.

These are: rolled cookies
You will need: greased cookie sheet

1 pint lard*
1 cup brown sugar
1 cup granulated sugar
2 eggs
½ teaspoon salt
1 teaspoon ground ginger
2 tablespoons baking soda
1 pint molasses
1 cup cold water
6 to 8 cups flour
Additional granulated sugar

**If you wish to substitute vegetable shortening, increase*
amount by ½ cup.

Preheat oven to 400°F.

Cream together lard and sugars. Beat in eggs, salt, ginger, and baking soda. Add molasses and water and beat again. Stir in enough flour to make a dough stiff enough to roll out. Roll out ¼ inch thick and sprinkle dough with granulated sugar. Cut out circles about 3½ inches in diameter. (Elizabeth Burgett uses a water glass to cut out the cookies.) Bake on a lightly greased cookie sheet for 8 to 10 minutes. They are done when you can press down with a finger and not leave a dent. Cool on wire racks.

Yield: about 6 dozen

Elizabeth Burgett
Muncy,
Pennsylvania
Lycoming
County Fair

Old-Fashioned Molasses Cookies

These are: rolled cookies
You will need: ungreased cookie sheet

1 cup vegetable shortening
1 cup sugar
1 cup molasses
1 cup hot water
2 tablespoons vinegar
4 teaspoons baking soda
1 teaspoon cinnamon
1 teaspoon vanilla extract
5 cups flour, approximately

Preheat oven to 350°F.

Melt the shortening and combine with sugar and molasses in a large mixing bowl. In a separate bowl, combine water and vinegar and stir in baking soda. Add to shortening mixture and mix well. Mix in cinnamon, vanilla, and enough flour to make a dough stiff enough to roll out. Roll out ¼ inch thick on a lightly floured surface and cut out desired shapes. Bake on ungreased cookie sheet for about 9 minutes, until edges are crisp and center is still soft. Cover with a towel until cookies are cooled.

Yield: about 4 dozen

Jean Young
Pataskala, Ohio
Ohio State Fair

Molasses Sugar Cookies

These are: molded cookies
You will need: greased cookie sheet

¼ pound plus 4 tablespoons butter
1 cup sugar
¼ cup molasses
1 egg
2 cups flour
2 teaspoons baking soda
½ teaspoon ground cloves
½ teaspoon ground ginger
1 teaspoon cinnamon
½ teaspoon salt
Additional sugar for topping

Preheat oven to 350°F.

Melt the butter, let cool a little, and add sugar, molasses, and egg. Sift together flour, baking soda, cloves, ginger, cinnamon, and salt. Stir into butter mixture. Roll into 1-inch balls and roll balls in sugar. Bake on a lightly greased cookie sheet for 8 to 10 minutes. Cool on wire racks.

Yield: 3½ to 4 dozen

Gayle Okonek
Myrtle Creek,
Oregon
Douglas
County Fair

Moravian Cookies

A traditional Christmas cookie to make in quantity. They last a long time in an airtight container.

These are: rolled cookies
You will need: greased cookie sheet

¾ cup vegetable shortening
¼ pound plus 4 tablespoons margarine
1 pound brown sugar
1 quart molasses
2 heaping tablespoons baking soda, dissolved in
½ cup boiling water
14 cups (4 pounds sifted flour), approximately
2 tablespoons cinnamon
2 tablespoons ground ginger
2 tablespoons ground cloves

Preheat oven to 300°F.

Melt vegetable shortening and margarine and set aside to cool. Put the brown sugar in a large mixing bowl and mash out the lumps. Add the melted shortening and mix well. Add the molasses and mix well. Beat in the baking soda solution. Sift together 2 cups of flour and the cinnamon, ginger, and cloves. Stir into liquid ingredients and continue adding flour, 1 cup at a time, until the dough is stiff and leaves the sides of the bowl. On a lightly floured surface, roll out the dough to ⅛ inch. Cut out designs with cookie cutters. Bake on a well-greased cookie sheet for about 10 minutes. Cool on wire racks. If cookies are soft when they are cool, they are not done. Test first batch and increase baking time for subsequent batches if necessary. Cookies should be very crisp.

Mrs. Kenneth
Sapp
Winston-Salem,
North Carolina
Dixie Classic Fair

Yield: about 8 pounds (about 500 cookies)

No-Bake Chocolate Oatmeal Cookies

These are: unbaked drop cookies
You will need: sheets of wax paper

2 cups sugar
½ cup cocoa
4 tablespoons butter
½ cup milk
½ cup peanut butter
1 teaspoon vanilla extract
3 cups rolled oats

Place sugar, cocoa, butter, and milk in a saucepan. Bring to a boil, stirring mixture continuously. Add the peanut butter, vanilla, and oatmeal. Stir well and remove from heat. Drop by teaspoonfuls onto wax paper. Let cool and harden.

Yield: 2½ to 3 dozen

Becky Miller
Beaverton,
Michigan
Gladwin
County Fair

No-Bake Peanut Butter Cookies

These are: bar cookies
You will need: greased 9 × 13-inch pan

12 graham crackers
1 cup peanut butter
2 cups confectioners' sugar
¼ pound butter, melted
1 12-ounce package sweetened chocolate chips
¼ cup heavy cream
1 tablespoon butter
1 cup walnuts, chopped

Crush the graham crackers and put into a large mixing bowl. Add the peanut butter, confectioners' sugar, and melted butter. Mix well and press into a greased 9 × 13-inch pan.

Combine chocolate chips, cream, and butter in the top of a double boiler and heat until the chocolate is melted. Pour over the graham cracker-peanut butter mixture and top with a layer of walnuts. When chocolate has hardened, cut into squares.

Yield: about 32

Sharon
Lee Shimmin
Salem, Oregon
Oregon State Fair

Oatmeal Cookies

These are: molded cookies
You will need: greased cookie sheet

½ **pound butter, at room temperature**
1 **cup granulated sugar**
1 **cup brown sugar**
2 **eggs**
2 **very ripe bananas, mashed**
1 **teaspoon vanilla extract**
1 ½ **cups flour**
1 **teaspoon salt**
1 **teaspoon baking soda**
1 **teaspoon baking powder**
2½ **cups quick-cooking oats**
Additional granulated sugar for topping

Preheat oven to 350°F.

Cream together the butter and sugars until light and fluffy. Beat in the eggs, mashed bananas, and vanilla. Sift together flour, salt, baking soda, and baking powder. Stir into creamed mixture and stir in oats. Form into small balls and roll in sugar. Bake on a greased cookie sheet, 2 inches apart, for 10 to 12 minutes. Cool on wire racks.

Yield: about 4 dozen

Mary B. Heying
Miami, Missouri
Missouri State Fair
Sedalia, Missouri

Crisp Oatmeal Cookies

These are: refrigerator cookies
You will need: greased cookie sheet

1 cup vegetable shortening
1 cup brown sugar
1 cup granulated sugar
2 eggs
1 teaspoon vanilla extract
1½ cups flour
1 teaspoon baking soda
1 teaspoon salt
3 cups quick-cooking oats
½ cup chopped nuts

Cream together the shortening and sugars. Beat in eggs and vanilla. Sift together flour, baking soda, and salt. Stir into creamed mixture. Stir in oatmeal, ½ cup at a time, mixing thoroughly with each addition. Stir in nuts. Divide dough in half and roll out each portion into a long log about 2 inches in diameter. Wrap and chill in refrigerator for several hours or overnight.

Preheat oven to 350°F.

Cut into thin slices, ⅛ to ¼ inch thick. Bake on a lightly greased cookie sheet, for 10 to 15 minutes, until lightly browned. Cool on wire racks.

Yield: 4 to 5 dozen

Susan R. Peterson
St. Croix Falls,
Wisconsin
Polk County Fair

Oatmeal Trilbys

Oatmeal cookie sandwiches with a date filling.

These are: refrigerator cookies with sandwich filling
You will need: greased cookie sheet

1¼ cups flour, sifted
1 teaspoon baking soda
¼ teaspoon salt
1 cup vegetable shortening
1 cup brown sugar
¼ cup hot water
2 cups quick-cooking oats

Sift together flour, baking soda, and salt. Cream together shortening and sugar until light and fluffy. Stir in dry ingredients alternately with hot water. Stir in oats. Divide dough in half and roll into logs 1½ to 2 inches in diameter. Wrap in plastic and refrigerate until firm (4 hours or longer).

Preheat oven to 375°F.

Cut dough into ¼-inch slices. Bake on a lightly greased cookie sheet for 10 to 12 minutes. Cool on wire racks. Spread with date filling to make sandwiches.

Date Filling

½ pound finely chopped dates
½ cup water
½ cup sugar
1 tablespoon lemon juice
¼ cup finely chopped nuts

Cook dates, water, and sugar over medium heat until mixture is thick. Stir in lemon juice and nuts. Cool thoroughly before making cookie sandwiches.

Lois Auernheimer
Fresno, California
Fresno District Fair

Yield: 2½ to 3 dozen

Rolled Oat Goodies

These are: molded cookies
You will need: ungreased cookie sheet

1 cup vegetable shortening
2 cups brown sugar
2 eggs
1 teaspoon vanilla extract
2½ cups flour
2 teaspoons baking soda
1 teaspoon salt
2 cups rolled oats
1 cup raisins
1 cup shredded coconut

Preheat oven to 350°F.

Cream together shortening and sugar until fluffy. Beat in eggs, one at a time, and vanilla. Sift together flour, baking soda, and salt. Stir into creamed mixture. Stir in rolled oats and raisins. Stir in shredded coconut. Shape into balls about 2 inches in diameter or dip with a #40 scoop. Bake on an ungreased cookie sheet, 2 inches apart, for 15 to 20 minutes. Cool on wire racks.

Yield: about 3 dozen

Kathleen Howe
Deland, Florida
Volusia
County Fair

Oatmeal-Raisin Cookies

These are: drop cookies
You will need: greased cookie sheet

⅔ cup butter or margarine, at room temperature
½ cup brown sugar
6 tablespoons granulated sugar
2 eggs
1 teaspoon vanilla extract
1½ cups rolled oats
1 cup flour
¾ teaspoon baking soda
½ teaspoon salt
1 cup raisins
½ cup semisweet chocolate pieces
½ cup chopped walnuts

Preheat oven to 350°F.

Cream together butter and both sugars until light and fluffy. Beat in eggs and vanilla extract. Combine oats, flour, baking soda, and salt and add to creamed mixture. Beat until thoroughly blended. Stir in raisins, chocolate pieces, and walnuts. Drop by rounded teaspoonfuls onto a greased cookie sheet, leaving 2 inches between each cookie. Bake for 10 to 12 minutes, until golden. Cool on wire racks.

Yield: 3 dozen

Faith Carlson
Malden, Illinois
Bureau County Fair

Orange Drop Cookies

These are: drop cookies
You will need: greased cookie sheet

½ **pound butter, softened to room temperature**
2 **cups sugar**
2 **eggs, beaten**
1 **cup sour milk or buttermilk**
Juice and grated rind of 1 orange
4½ **cups flour**
1 **teaspoon baking soda**
1 **teaspoon baking powder**
¼ **teaspoon salt**

Preheat oven to 350°F.

Cream together butter and sugar. Beat in eggs, sour milk, and orange juice and rind. Sift together flour, baking soda, baking powder, and salt. Add to liquid ingredients and beat well. Drop by teaspoonfuls onto a lightly greased cookie sheet and bake for 8 to 10 minutes. Cool on wire racks.

Yield: approximately 8 dozen

Dolores Millward
Coshocton, Ohio
Coshocton
County Fair

Peanut Butter Cookies I

These are: molded cookies
You will need: ungreased cookie sheet

¼ pound butter, softened to room temperature
½ cup (or a little more) freshly ground
    peanut butter*
⅓ cup granulated sugar
½ cup brown sugar
1 egg
½ teaspoon vanilla extract
1¼ cups sifted flour
¾ teaspoon baking soda
⅛ teaspoon salt
½ cup toasted peanut halves

Freshly ground peanut butter can be purchased in most health food stores. Or you can make your own in an electric blender or food processor. To 1 cup peanuts add 1½ to 2 tablespoons of vegetable oil. Process to desired consistency and add salt to taste.

Preheat oven to 375°F.

Cream together thoroughly the butter, peanut butter, and both sugars. Beat in egg and vanilla. Sift together flour, baking soda, and salt. Blend into creamed mixture. Shape into 1-inch balls and arrange on an ungreased cookie sheet. Crisscross tops with the tines of a fork to slightly flatten cookies. Bake for 8 to 10 minutes. Remove from oven and press 4 peanut halves atop each cookie as decoration. Cool on wire racks.

Carolyn G. Plante
Ceres, California
Stanislaus
County Fair
Alameda
County Fair

Yield: 2½ dozen

Peanut Butter Cookies II

"We live on a farm and have five married children and fourteen grandchildren," writes Shirley Pattee. "They all live close by and so help get rid of my excess baking. I help in the fields, especially during harvest, driving a tractor and bringing in the loads of corn and beans."

These are: molded cookies
You will need: greased cookie sheet

1 cup butter-flavored vegetable shortening
¾ cup peanut butter
1 cup granulated sugar
1 cup brown sugar
2 eggs
1 teaspoon vanilla extract
2 tablespoons hot water
½ teaspoon butter flavoring
3 cups flour (more if needed)
2 teaspoons baking powder
½ teaspoon salt

Preheat oven to 350°F.

Cream together the vegetable shortening, peanut butter, and both sugars. Beat in the eggs, vanilla, hot water, and flavorings. Sift together flour, baking powder, and salt. Stir into creamed mixture. Roll into 1-inch balls and arrange on a lightly greased cookie sheet, 2 inches apart. Press down on cookies with the tines of a fork and bake for 10 minutes. Cool on wire racks.

Yield: 6 to 7 dozen

Shirley B. Pattee
Shelby, Iowa
East Pattawattamie
County Fair

Chippy Peanut Butter Cookies

These are: molded cookies
You will need: ungreased cookie sheet

¾ pound butter, softened to room temperature
1½ cups peanut butter
1½ cups granulated sugar
1½ cups brown sugar
3 eggs, beaten
1 teaspoon vanilla extract
3¾ cups flour
2¼ teaspoons baking soda
1½ teaspoons baking powder
¾ teaspoon salt
18 ounces peanut butter chips

Cream together the butter, peanut butter, and both sugars until smooth. Beat in the eggs and vanilla. Sift together flour, baking soda, baking powder, and salt. Stir into creamed mixture and blend well. Stir in peanut butter chips. Chill in refrigerator for 30 minutes.

Preheat oven to 350°F.

Shape dough into 1-inch balls and arrange on ungreased cookie sheets, 2 inches apart. Press down on each cookie with the tines of a fork. Bake for 10 to 12 minutes (10 for chewy, 12 for crisp).

Yield: 5 to 6 dozen

Doris Swank
Naples, Florida
Florida State Fair
Collier County Fair
Southwest
Florida Fair

Peanut Butter Crunchies

These are: molded cookies
You will need: greased cookie sheet

½ pound butter, softened to room temperature
⅔ cup chunky peanut butter
1 cup brown sugar
1 egg
1 teaspoon vanilla extract
1⅓ cups flour
½ teaspoon baking soda
¼ teaspoon salt
¾ cup crushed Wheaties

Cream together butter, peanut butter, and sugar until light and fluffy. Beat in egg and vanilla. Sift together flour, baking soda, and salt. Stir into creamed mixture. Refrigerate dough for several hours, until firm.

Preheat oven to 350°F.

Shape dough into 1-inch balls and roll in crushed Wheaties. Place balls 2 inches apart on a lightly greased cookie sheet. Bake 12 to 15 minutes. Cool on wire racks.

Yield: 4 dozen

Laura Case York
Valrico, Florida
Florida State Fair

Peanut Butter Jam Cookies

These are: filled refrigerator cookies
You will need: ungreased cookie sheet

1½ cups sifted flour
½ cup sugar
1 teaspoon baking soda
¼ teaspoon salt
½ cup vegetable shortening
½ cup creamy peanut butter
¼ cup light corn syrup
1 tablespoon milk
Strawberry jam and crunchy peanut butter

Sift together flour, sugar, baking soda, and salt. Cut in shortening and peanut butter until mixture resembles coarse meal. Blend in syrup and milk. Shape into a log 2 inches in diameter, wrap in plastic, and chill until firm (4 to 12 hours).

Preheat oven to 350°F.

Slice ⅛ to ¼ inch thick. Place half the slices on an ungreased cookie sheet. Spread each slice with ¼ teaspoon jam and ½ teaspoon crunchy peanut butter. Cover with remaining slices and seal edges with the tines of a fork. Bake for 7 to 10 minutes. Cool slightly before removing to wire racks.

Yield: 2 dozen

Ruth B. Ekberg
Reedley, California
Fresno District Fair

Peanut Kisses

"My late mother-in-law baked a peanut cookie with a chocolate kiss center, which my husband dearly loves," says Mary Spangler. Now Mrs. Spangler bakes them and says that, "these cookies are a big hit with children of all ages."

These are: molded cookies
You will need: ungreased cookie sheet

2¾ cups unbleached flour
1 cup brown sugar
1 cup chunky peanut butter (the chunkier the better)
½ pound butter or margarine, softened to room temperature
¾ cup granulated sugar
1½ teaspoons baking soda
1 teaspoon salt
1 teaspoon vanilla extract
2 large eggs, at room temperature
Additional granulated sugar
8 dozen chocolate kisses, unwrapped

Preheat oven to 350°F.

Measure all the ingredients except additional sugar and kisses into a large bowl. Mix well to blend completely. Shape dough into 1-inch balls. Use a melon scoop to make dough balls a uniform size. Roll dough balls in sugar and place them about 2 inches apart on ungreased cookie sheets. Bake for 12 minutes. Remove from oven and press a chocolate kiss in the center of each cookie. Return to oven and bake 1 minute more. Cool on wire racks.

Mary W. Spangler
Kernersville,
North Carolina
Dixie Classic Fair

Yield: 7 to 8 dozen

Pecan Butter Balls

These are: molded cookies
You will need: ungreased cookie sheet

¼ cup sugar
½ pound butter, softened to room temperature
2 teaspoons vanilla extract
2 cups flour
½ teaspoon salt
2 cups finely chopped pecans
Confectioners' sugar

Preheat oven to 325°F.

Cream together sugar and butter until light and fluffy. Beat in vanilla. Add flour and salt and blend to a soft, smooth dough. Stir in pecans. Shape into 1-inch balls. Place 2 inches apart on an ungreased cookie sheet. Bake for 25 minutes, until cookies are firm and light brown on the bottom. Remove from cookie sheet and roll in confectioners' sugar. Cool on wire racks. Store in an airtight container.

Yield: about 3 dozen

Doris Swank
Naples, Florida
Collier County Fair

Polvorones
(Powder Puff Cookies)

"This recipe was given to me by a cousin in Mexico City," writes Lucretia Thornburg. "I decided that the pink powder puff cookie would look more like its name if I sprinkled some powdered sugar on it. I won a blue ribbon in the Foreign Cookie division with this recipe."

These are: rolled cookies
You will need: ungreased cookie sheet

¾ cup plus 2 tablespoons lard
½ cup sugar
Few drops of red food coloring
1 egg yolk
2½ cups flour
¼ teaspoon cinnamon
¼ teaspoon salt
Confectioners' sugar

Preheat oven to 350°F.

Cream together lard and sugar until fluffy. Add red food coloring. Beat in egg yolk. Sift together flour, cinnamon, and salt and stir into lard mixture. Mix thoroughly. Roll out dough ⅓ inch thick and cut out cookies with a 2½-inch circular cutter. Bake on ungreased cookie sheet for 12 to 15 minutes. Cool on wire racks. Sprinkle confectioners' sugar on cookies with a sifter. This is what makes them look like a pink powder puff.

Yield: 2½ dozen

Lucretia Thornburg
Mojave, California
Antelope
Valley Fair

Potato Chip Cookies

These are: drop cookies
You will need: ungreased cookie sheet

1 pound butter or margarine (margarine makes them crisper), softened to room temperature
1¼ cups sugar
2 teaspoons vanilla extract
3½ cups flour
1½ cups crushed potato chips
Confectioners' sugar

Preheat oven to 350°F.

Cream together butter or margarine and sugar. Beat in vanilla. Blend in flour. Fold in potato chips. Drop by teaspoonfuls on ungreased cookie sheets. Bake for 12 to 14 minutes. Dust with confectioners' sugar. Cool on wire racks.

Note: At holiday time colored crystal sugar can be sprinkled on top of the powdered sugar.

Yield: about 5 dozen

Ruth Lundberg
Auburn, California
Gold Country Fair
California
State Fair

Powdered Sugar Cookies

This recipe has been in the Schneiderman family for years.

These are: molded cookies
You will need: greased cookie sheet

½ pound butter, softened to room temperature
1 cup confectioners' sugar
1 egg
1 teaspoon vanilla extract
2 cups flour
½ teaspoon baking soda

Preheat oven to 350°F.

Cream the butter until light and fluffy. Beat in confectioners' sugar, then the egg and vanilla extract. Sift together flour and baking soda and stir into creamed mixture. Shape into 1-inch balls and arrange 2 inches apart on a lightly greased cookie sheet. Press each ball down with the tines of a fork. Bake for about 6 minutes. Cool on wire racks.

Yield: about 5 dozen

Louise
Schneiderman
Bottineau,
North Dakota
Bottineau
County Fair

Pressed Cookies

Mrs. Allred has been making these cookies for more than thirty years and winning prizes in fairs all over North Carolina.

These are: pressed cookies
You will need: ungreased cookie sheet

¼ pound butter, softened to room temperature
½ cup sugar
1 egg yolk
½ teaspoon vanilla extract
1½ cups cake flour
½ teaspoon baking powder
⅛ teaspoon salt
3 teaspoons evaporated milk or cream

Preheat oven to 400°F.

Cream butter and sugar together and beat well. Stir in the egg yolk and vanilla. Sift together flour, baking powder, and salt and add to other ingredients. Mix well. Place into a cookie press and press onto an ungreased cookie sheet, leaving about 2 inches between each cookie. Bake for 8 to 10 minutes, or until the edges are lightly brown.

Yield: About 6 dozen

Mrs. Edward
Allred
Lexington,
North Carolina
Davidson County
Agricultural Fair
Dixie Classic Fair
North Carolina
State Fair

Pride of Iowa Cookies

These are: drop cookies
You will need: greased cookie sheet

1 cup brown sugar
1 cup granulated sugar
1 cup vegetable shortening
2 eggs
2 cups flour
½ teaspoon salt
1 teaspoon baking soda
1 teaspoon baking powder
1 teaspoon vanilla extract
1 cup flaked coconut
3 cups rolled oats
½ cup chopped nuts

Preheat oven to 375°F.

Cream together sugars and shortening until light and fluffy. Beat in eggs. Sift together flour, salt, baking soda, and baking powder. Stir into creamed mixture. Stir in vanilla, coconut, oats, and nuts. Mix well and drop by teaspoonfuls onto a greased cookie sheet. Flatten by pressing down with the bottom of a glass. Bake for about 8 minutes, until cookies are light brown. Cool on wire racks.

Yield: about 4 dozen

Helen L. Hannon
Kouts, Indiana
Porter County Fair

Pumpkin Chocolate Chip Cookies

These are: drop cookies
You will need: ungreased cookie sheet

1 cup vegetable shortening
1½ cups sugar
3 eggs
1 cup canned pumpkin
½ cup hot water
4 cups flour
1 teaspoon salt
1 teaspoon baking soda
1 teaspoon baking powder
1 teaspoon cinnamon
12 ounces chocolate chips

Preheat oven to 350°F.

Cream together shortening and sugar until smooth. Beat in eggs, one at a time, then the pumpkin and water. Beat until smooth. Sift together flour, salt, baking soda, baking powder, and cinnamon. Fold in chocolate chips. Drop by teaspoonfuls, 2 inches apart, onto an ungreased cookie sheet and bake for 15 minutes. Cool on wire racks.

Yield: about 5 dozen

Kim Christenson
Amarillo, Texas
State Fair of Texas

Pumpkin Cookies

These are: drop cookies
You will need: ungreased cookie sheet

3 cups sugar
5 to 6 teaspoons pumpkin pie spices
6 teaspoons baking powder
1½ teaspoons baking soda
1 teaspoon salt
2½ cups canned pumpkin
1 cup vegetable oil
2 eggs, beaten lightly
1 teaspoon vanilla extract
5 cups flour

Preheat oven to 350°F.

Combine sugar, spices, baking powder, baking soda, and salt. Mix well and reserve. Mix together pumpkin, vegetable oil, eggs, and vanilla. Blend the sugar mixture into the pumpkin mixture. Gradually blend in flour. Drop by teaspoonfuls, 2 inches apart, onto an ungreased cookie sheet and bake for 15 to 20 minutes. Cool on wire racks.

Yield: 9 to 10 dozen

Patricia Leinweber
Phoenix, Arizona
Arizona State Fair

Raisin Bran Cookies

These are: drop cookies
You will need: greased cookie sheet

¼ pound margarine, at room temperature
½ cup brown sugar
¼ cup granulated sugar
1 egg
1 teaspoon vanilla extract
1 tablespoon milk
1 cup flour
½ teaspoon baking powder
½ teaspoon baking soda
1 cup 100% bran cereal
½ cup chopped nuts
¾ cup raisins

Preheat oven to 350°F.

Cream together margarine and sugars until smooth and creamy. Beat in egg, vanilla, and milk until fluffy. Sift together flour, baking powder, and baking soda and mix with cereal. Stir into creamed mixture until well blended. Stir in nuts and raisins. Drop by teaspoonfuls onto a greased cookie sheet. Bake for 10 to 13 minutes, until lightly browned. Cool on wire racks.

Yield: 3½ dozen

Patricia A. Semrick
Fresno, California
Fresno County Fair

Raisin-Filled Cookies

"This is my mother's recipe," writes Alberta Fahrenbach. "I helped her bake when I was still at home. My family at that time was eight brothers and four sisters. We were a farm family and it took a lot of cooking and baking to keep us fed. Now I have five grandchildren and I live on my husband's grandparents' farm and I still do all my own baking. Neither my husband nor I can eat store-bought bread or cookies."

These are: filled rolled cookies
You will need: greased cookie sheet

2 cups sugar
1 cup vegetable shortening
2 eggs
1 teaspoon vanilla extract
6 cups flour
2 teaspoons cream of tartar
2 teaspoons baking soda
1 teaspoon salt
1 cup sour cream

Raisin Filling
3 cups raisins
2 tablespoons flour
1 cup sugar
1½ cups water

Cream together sugar and shortening until light and fluffy. Beat in eggs and vanilla. Sift together 5 cups of flour, cream of tartar, baking soda, and salt. Reserve 1 cup of flour for rolling out the dough. Stir into creamed mixture alternately with sour cream to make a soft dough. Add more flour only if necessary to make dough hold together. Chill dough in refrigerator until firm.

Meanwhile, prepare the filling. Mix raisins with flour and sugar. Combine with water in a saucepan and cook over moderate heat until raisins are plumped and mixture has thickened. Remove from heat and let cool.

Preheat oven to 350°F.

On a lightly floured board or pastry cloth, roll out chilled dough to ⅛-inch thickness. Cut out with a round cookie cutter and place on a lightly greased cookie sheet. Place a heaping teaspoon of raisin filling on each round of dough and top with another circle of dough. Press edges together with fingers. Bake for 10 to 15 minutes, or until lightly browned. Cool on wire racks.

Yield: 3 to 4 dozen

Alberta
Fahrenbach
Muncy,
Pennsylvania
Hughsville Fair

Raisin Scotchie Bars

These are: bar cookies
You will need: greased 8 × 8-inch pan

¼ pound butter or margarine, at
   room temperature
¾ cup sugar
1 egg
½ teaspoon vanilla extract
½ teaspoon almond extract
½ teaspoon baking powder
1 cup flour
½ cup quick-cooking rolled oats
½ cup raisins
½ cup crushed cornflakes
6 ounces butterscotch morsels

Preheat oven to 350°F.

Cream butter and sugar until light and fluffy. Beat in egg and vanilla and almond extracts. Sift together baking powder and flour. Stir into creamed mixture and mix well. Stir in oats, raisins, cornflakes, and butterscotch morsels. Spread in a greased 8 × 8-inch pan. Bake for 20 minutes. Cool. Cut into bars.

Yield: 32

Ruth B. Ekberg
Reedley, California
Fresno District Fair

Raisin Wheat Bars

These are: bar cookies
You will need: greased 7 × 11-inch pan

¼ pound butter or margarine, at
    room temperature
½ cup sugar
1 egg
½ teaspoon lemon juice
1¼ cups sifted flour
½ teaspoon baking soda
¼ teaspoon salt
1 tablespoon wheat germ
2 tablespoons grated mild cheese
½ cup raisins

Preheat oven to 350°F.

Cream together butter and sugar until light and fluffy. Beat in egg and lemon juice. Sift together flour, baking soda, and salt and stir into creamed mixture. Mix in wheat germ, cheese, and raisins. Spread in a greased 7 × 11-inch pan. Bake for 15 minutes. Cool in pan and cut into bars.

Yield: About 2½ dozen

Ruth B. Ekberg
Reedley, California
Fresno District Fair

Raspberry Jewels

Dr. Marilyn Kurnath is a history instructor at the Cleveland School of Science. A family favorite, her cookie recipe took top prize at the Cuyahoga County Fair. "We only use sweet butter in our cookies; we don't use any salt in them at all." Mrs. Kurnath believes in using only top-quality ingredients, and the filling for these cookies was made from her own home-grown raspberries. "The size is also very important," she writes. "The secret is not to have gigantic cookies, but cookies that are very neat and uniform."

These are: molded, filled cookies
You will need: ungreased cookie sheet

¼ pound butter, softened to room temperature
¼ cup dark brown sugar
1 egg yolk, beaten
½ teaspoon vanilla extract
1 cup sifted flour
1 egg white
1½ cups walnuts, coarsely chopped
Raspberry jam, preferably homemade

Preheat oven to 350 degrees.

In a mixing bowl, cream together butter and brown sugar until fluffy. Add egg yolk and vanilla; beat well. Gradually add sifted flour until dough is well mixed. Gather into a ball.

Pinch off pieces of dough and roll into balls about 1 inch in diameter. Place egg white and nuts in separate plates. Roll each ball in egg white and then in nuts until well coated. Arrange balls on ungreased cookie sheets. Flatten each slightly with the palm of the hand, then make a depression with the thumb in the center. Bake for 8 minutes. Open oven; quickly make depressions again (use glove if necessary to keep from burning). Close oven; bake about 10 minutes more, or until lightly browned around edges. Remove to wire racks and let cool thoroughly. Fill each depression with raspberry jam.

Yield: about 16

Dr. Marilyn Kurnath Middlebury Heights, Ohio Cuyahoga County Fair

Raspberry Squares

These are: rolled cookies
You will need: greased cookie sheet

4 cups flour
1⅓ cups vegetable shortening
8 to 10 tablespoons cold water
2 cups fresh raspberries
1½ cups sugar

Mix together flour, shortening, and water as for a pie crust. Cut shortening into flour until mixture resembles small peas. Add enough water to make pastry stick together. Roll into a ball, wrap in plastic, and refrigerate for 30 minutes.

Mix raspberries and sugar together in a bowl and let rest at least 15 minutes. Drain the berries in a sieve. Use juice for another purpose.

Preheat oven to 400°F.

Divide pastry dough in half and roll out half of dough on a lightly floured surface to an 8 × 10-inch rectangle. Transfer to a greased cookie sheet. Spread raspberries on rolled out pastry dough. Roll out the remaining pastry and cover the raspberries. Cut slits all over top crust to allow steam to escape. Sprinkle top crust with 1 teaspoon sugar. Bake for 30 to 40 minutes. Allow to cool in pan, then cut into 2 × 1-inch rectangles.

Yield: about 40

Note: You can substitute 1½ cups raspberry jam for the fresh raspberries, in which case you should omit the sugar.

Debbie Austin
Westmoreland,
New Hampshire
Cheshire Fair

Sesame Crisps

These are: refrigerator cookies
You will need: ungreased cookie sheet

½ **pound butter, at room temperature**
¾ **cup sugar**
1½ **cups flour**
½ **cup sesame seeds**
1 **cup shredded coconut**
¼ **cup finely chopped almonds**

Cream the butter. Gradually beat in sugar and beat until mixture is light and fluffy. Add flour and mix until just combined. Stir in sesame seeds, coconut, and almonds, just until well mixed. Chill dough for 30 minutes. Pack dough into empty, topless and bottomless 6-ounce juice cans, or roll into logs and wrap in plastic. Refrigerate until firm.

Preheat oven to 300°F.

Cut dough into slices ¼ inch thick. If dough is in juice cans, push dough out of cans at ¼-inch intervals and slice. Bake on ungreased cookie sheets for 30 minutes, or until just golden brown around the edges. Cool on wire racks.

Yield: 2 dozen

Ursula Maurer
Wauwatosa,
Wisconsin
Wisconsin State
Fair

Snow-White Cookies

These are: molded cookies
You will need: ungreased cookie sheet

¾ pound butter or margarine, softened to
   room temperature
1 cup sugar
2 eggs
4 teaspoons vanilla extract
4 cups flour
1 teaspoon salt
12 ounces chocolate chips
2 cups walnuts, chopped
Confectioners' sugar, sifted

Cream together butter and sugar until light and fluffy. Beat in eggs and vanilla. Sift together flour and salt. Blend into creamed mixture. Fold in chocolate chips and walnuts. Chill in refrigerator until firm.

Preheat oven to 350°F.

Roll dough into 1-inch balls and place on an ungreased cookie sheet 2 inches apart. Bake for 15 to 20 minutes. Cool on wire racks. When completely cool, roll in sifted confectioners' sugar.

Yield: about 7 dozen

Cindee Tine
Middletown,
Connecticut
Durham Fair

Old-Fashioned Sour Cream Drops

These are: drop cookies
You will need: ungreased cookie sheet

½ cup vegetable shortening
1½ cups sugar
2 eggs
1 cup sour cream
1 teaspoon vanilla extract
2¾ cups sifted flour
1 teaspoon baking powder
1 teaspoon salt
1 teaspoon baking soda

Cream together the shortening and sugar. Beat the eggs lightly and blend into sugar mixture. Stir in sour cream and vanilla. Sift flour, baking powder, salt, and baking soda together and stir into creamed mixture. Cover and chill in refrigerator 1 hour or longer.

Preheat oven to 400°F.

Drop cookie mixture by teaspoonfuls, 2 inches apart, onto an ungreased cookie sheet. Bake for 8 to 10 minutes. Cool on wire racks.

Yield: about 4 dozen

Dorothy Spencer
Orlando, Florida
Central
Florida Fair

Spritz Cookies

The name for these cookies comes from the German word "spritzen," meaning, "to squirt," because the soft dough is pushed, or squirted, through a cookie press to make fancy designs.

These are: pressed cookies
You will need: ungreased cookie sheet

½ pound butter, softened to room temperature
⅔ cup sugar
1 egg, beaten
1 teaspoon almond extract
2½ cups flour
½ teaspoon baking powder

Preheat oven to 375°F.

Cream together butter and sugar until light and fluffy. Beat in egg and almond extract. Sift together flour and baking powder and stir into creamed mixture. Pack in a cookie press and press out onto an ungreased cookie sheet, spacing cookies 1 inch apart. Bake for 8 to 10 minutes. Cool on wire racks.

Yield: about 5 dozen

Nancy R.
Winklepleck
Atwater, California
Merced County Fair

Crispy Sugar Cookies

Make the dough the day before you bake the cookies.

These are: rolled cookies
You will need: greased cookie sheet

¼ pound butter, softened to room temperature
¾ cup sugar
1 tablespoon heavy cream
1 teaspoon almond extract
1¼ cups flour
¼ teaspoon baking powder
¼ teaspoon salt
Additional granulated sugar for topping

Cream together the butter, sugar, heavy cream, and almond extract until light and fluffy. Sift together the flour, baking powder, and salt. Fold the flour mixture into the butter mixture. Refrigerate overnight.

Preheat oven to 425°F.

Roll the dough out very thin on a lightly floured surface. Cut out desired shapes with a cookie cutter and place on a lightly greased cookie sheet. Sprinkle with additional sugar. Bake for 5 to 7 minutes. Cool on wire racks.

Yield: about 2½ dozen

Mary B. Heying
Miami, Missouri
Missouri State Fair

Old-Fashioned Sugar Cookies

These are: rolled cookies
You will need: greased cookie sheet

2½ to 3 cups sifted cake flour
2 teaspoons baking powder
½ teaspoon salt
¼ pound butter, softened to room temperature
1 cup sugar
2 eggs, well beaten
1 teaspoon vanilla extract
    or
½ teaspoon lemon extract

Sift together flour, baking powder, and salt. Cream butter and sugar until light and fluffy. Add eggs and beat well. Add vanilla or lemon extract. Add flour gradually, stirring it in, until dough leaves the sides of the bowl. Chill 15 minutes or longer.

Preheat oven to 375°F.

Roll out dough on a lightly floured surface and cut with 3-inch cookie cutters dipped in flour. Bake on a greased cookie sheet for 8 to 10 minutes. Cookies should be firm but not brown. Cool on wire racks.

Yield: 3 dozen

Edith H. Leet
Albany, New York
The Altamont Fair

Quick Crisp
Sugar Cookies

These are: rolled cookies
You will need: greased cookie sheet

2¼ cups sifted flour
½ teaspoon baking soda
1 teaspoon baking powder
½ teaspoon salt
¼ pound butter, softened to room temperature
1 cup sugar
2 eggs
1 teaspoon vanilla extract
1 tablespoon milk
Additional granulated sugar for topping

Sift together flour, baking soda, baking powder, and salt and set aside. Cream the butter and sugar until light and fluffy. Beat in eggs, one at a time, then vanilla and milk. Fold flour mixture into creamed mixture. Wrap dough in wax paper and chill for about 2 hours, or roll out at once if preferred.

Preheat oven to 425°F.

Roll out dough on a lightly floured surface to ⅛-inch thickness. Cut with a cookie cutter that has been dipped in flour. Sprinkle with sugar. Bake for about 8 minutes, or until golden brown. Cool on wire racks. Brush with Sugar Icing, if desired.

Sugar Icing

1 pound confectioners' sugar
1 cup vegetable shortening
½ cup milk
1 teaspoon vanilla extract

Blend everything together to a spreadable consistency.

Yield: 2½ dozen

Jane Dempsey
Bethalta, Illinois
Illinois State Fair

Sugar Cookies

These are: rolled cookies
You will need: greased cookie sheet

2 eggs
3 cups sugar
1 cup sour cream
½ pound butter or margarine, at
    room temperature
2 tablespoons butternut flavoring, or 1 teaspoon
    each vanilla and almond extract
6 to 8 cups flour
1 heaping teaspoon baking soda
1 teaspoon baking powder
Additional granulated sugar for topping

Beat eggs and sugar until creamy. Blend in sour cream, butter, and butternut flavoring. Sift together 2 cups of flour, the baking soda, and baking powder. Blend flour into creamed mixture and add enough additional flour to make a soft dough that is not sticky. (The amount of flour depends upon the weather and humidity.) Chill the dough for a few hours, for easier handling.

Preheat oven to 350°F.

Roll out dough on a lightly floured surface until it is approximately ⅛-inch thick. Cut out desired shapes with cookie cutters. Sprinkle with granulated sugar. Bake on lightly greased cookie sheets for 10 to 15 minutes, or until they start to brown slightly. Cool on wire racks.

Yield: about 4 pounds (7 to 8 dozen)

Mrs. Kenneth
Sapp
Winston-Salem,
North Carolina
Dixie Classic Fair

Swedish Butter Cookies

These are: molded cookies
You will need: ungreased cookie sheet

½ **pound butter, softened to room temperature**
½ **cup sugar**
1 **egg yolk**
1 **tablespoon cream**
2 **cups flour**
¼ **teaspoon baking powder**
½ **teaspoon almond extract**
1 **egg white**
½ **cup chopped walnuts**
Raspberry jam for garnish

Preheat oven to 325°F.

Cream together butter and sugar until light and fluffy. Beat in egg yolk, cream, flour, baking powder, and almond flavoring.

Place unbeaten egg white in a saucer. Place nuts in another saucer. Shape dough into small balls, dip in egg white, then into nuts. Arrange on an ungreased cookie sheet and indent centers with thumb or forefinger. Bake 5 minutes and remove from oven. Check indentations and press again if necessary. Fill with a tiny amount of raspberry jam. Return to oven and bake 15 minutes more, or until cookies turn a light brown.

Yield: about 4 dozen

Ruth Lundberg
Auburn, California
Gold County Fair
California
State Fair

Swiss Chocolate Squares

These cookies are very moist and rich, like brownies.

These are: bar cookies
You will need: ungreased 15½ × 10-inch pan

1 cup water
¼ pound butter or margarine
6 squares (6 ounces) unsweetened chocolate
2 cups flour
2 cups sugar
2 eggs
½ cup sour cream
1 teaspoon baking soda
½ teaspoon salt

Preheat oven to 350°F.

Combine water, butter, and chocolate in a heavy saucepan or the top of a double boiler. Heat until chocolate is melted and mixture is smooth. Remove from heat and pour into large mixing bowl. Blend in remaining ingredients and mix well. Pour into an ungreased 15½ × 10-inch pan. Bake for 20 to 25 minutes. Remove pan to wire rack and cool.

Milk Chocolate Frosting

¼ pound butter or margarine
6 tablespoons milk
6 squares (6 ounces) unsweetened chocolate
4½ cups sifted confectioners' sugar
1 teaspoon vanilla extract
Pecan halves for garnish (optional)

Combine butter or margarine, milk, and chocolate in a saucepan. Heat until chocolate is melted and mixture is smooth. Remove from heat and pour into a large mixing bowl. Beat in the confectioners' sugar and beat until smooth. Stir in vanilla extract. Spread on uncut cookie dough and, when completely cooled, cut into squares. Garnish each cookie with a pecan half.

Yield: about 30

Margie Wagner
Mount Sterling,
Illinois
Brown County Fair
Schuyler Rushville
Fair

Old-Fashioned Tea Cakes

These are: rolled cookies
You will need: ungreased cookie sheet

1 egg
½ cup vegetable shortening
1 cup sugar
1 teaspoon baking soda
1 teaspoon salt
1 teaspoon buttermilk
1 teaspoon baking powder
1 teaspoon vanilla extract
1½ cups self-rising flour
Sugar for topping

Preheat oven to 325°F.

Mix together everything except the flour. Stir in flour just to mix and roll out the dough. Cut into desired shapes. Bake on ungreased cookie sheets for 12 minutes. Remove from oven and sprinkle tops with sugar before removing cookies from pan. Cool on wire racks.

Yield: 2 dozen

Sheila Womack
Fayetteville,
Tennessee
Lincoln
County Fair

Thumb-Print Cookies

These are: molded cookies
You will need: ungreased cookie sheet

¼ **pound butter, softened to room temperature**
¼ **cup brown sugar**
1 **egg, separated**
½ **teaspoon vanilla extract**
1 **cup flour**
¼ **teaspoon salt**
1 **cup finely chopped pecans**

Preheat oven to 350°F.

Cream together butter and sugar until light and fluffy. Beat in egg yolk and vanilla. Stir in flour and salt. Roll into 1-inch balls. Beat egg white slightly with a fork. Dip balls in egg white and roll in chopped nuts. Place 1 inch apart on an ungreased cookie sheet. Press thumb gently in the center of each cookie. Bake 8 to 10 minutes. Cool on wire racks. Fill cookies with icing if desired. Use rosette tip on decorating tube to fill cookies.

Icing   ½ **cup vegetable shortening**
¼ **pound butter**
2 **tablespoons boiling water**
¾ **tablespoon vanilla extract**
¾ **teaspoon salt**
½ **cup evaporated milk**
1 **pound confectioners' sugar**

Mix everything together until well blended. If too thin, add more confectioners' sugar. Can be kept in refrigerator for 2 weeks or longer.

Mrs. Joseph Ault
LaPorte, Indiana
LaPorte
County Fair

Yield: 3 dozen

Index

Heying, Mary B., 87, 119
High Fiber, Low Sugar Oatmeal Chews, 62–63
Holtin, Alice, 57
honey, 6
Honey Crinkle Cookies, 64
Honey Nut Bars, 65
Howe, Kathleen, 90
Hungarian Butter Horns, 66–67

Ice Box Cookies, 68
    see also refrigerator (ice box) cookies
ingredients, 6
Italian Sesame Sticks, 69
Italian Wedding Cookies, 70

Keller-Sherman, Karen, 40, 41
Kird, Christine C., 56
Kurnath, Dr. Marilyn, 112, 113

Leet, Edith H., 120
Leinweber, Patricia, 23, 106
Lelasher, Ellen A., 37
Lemon Bars, 71–72
Lemon Cookie Sandwiches, 73–74
Lemon Filling, 73–74
Lemon Glaze, 15
Long, Margaret, 42
Lundberg, Ruth, 101, 124

McQuain, Samantha, 38, 39
Mann, Laurel M., 30, 31
margarine, 6
Marshmallow, Chocolate Drops, 36
Marshmallow Fudge Bars, 74–75

Maurer, Ursula, 51, 62, 63, 115
measuring cups, spoons, 5
Milk Chocolate Frosting, 125–26
Miller, Becky, 85
Millward, Dolores, 92
Minnie's Pfeffernusse Cookies, 77–78
Mishler, Mrs. Merle, 35
mixer, electric, 5
mixing, 6
mixing bowls, 5
mixing spoons, scrapers, 5
molasses, 6
Molasses Cookies
    Drop, 79
    Old-Fashioned, 82
    Rolled, 90
    Sugar, 83
molded (shaped) cookies, 3–4
    testing for doneness, 7
Moravian cookies, 84

Neavoll, Fran, 53
No-Bake Chocolate Oatmeal Cookies, 85
No-Bake Peanut Butter Cookies, 86
nonstick-surface utensils, 4–5
nut cookies
    Brazil, Bars, 23
    Frosted Cashew, 32
    Honey, Bars, 65

Oat Cookies, Rolled, 90
Oatmeal Cookies, 87
    Apple, 10–11
    Crisp, 88